10

MINUTE GUIDE TO

HOUSEHOLD BUDGETING

by Tracey Longo

alpha books

Macmillan Spectrum/Alpha Books

A Division of Macmillan General Reference
A Simon and Schuster Macmillan Company
1633 Broadway, New York, NY 10019-6785

International Standard Book Number: 0-02-861442-9
Library of Congress Catalog Card Number: 96-078165

99 98 97   8 7 6 5 4 3 2 1

Interpretation of the printing code: the rightmost double-digit number is the year of the book's first printing; the rightmost single-digit number is the number of the book's printing. For example, a printing code of 97-1 shows that this copy of the book was printed during the first printing of the book in 1997.

Printed in the United States of America

Publisher: Theresa Murtha

Editor in Chief: Richard J. Staron

Production Editor: Michael Thomas

Copy Editor: Mike McFeely

Cover Designer: Dan Armstrong

Designer: Glenn Larsen

Indexers: Ginny Bess, Eric Brinkman

Production Team: Angela Calvert, Tricia Flodder, Mary Hunt, Christy Wagner, Maureen West

CONTENTS

INTRODUCTION

Ever wonder where your money goes every month? Hectic lifestyles and unexpected expenses can push developing and living by a household budget into last place on just about anyone's to-do list. This book is dedicated to helping you turn simple but effective budgeting into an integral part of your financial life so that you'll have cash left over—after you pay your bills—to save or invest each month.

If you're creating your first workable budget, this guide will help you break down your finances into manageable pieces, identify and curtail spending habits, and soundly project your financial needs so you can draw up a plan that enables you to accomplish your goals. If you already have a budget, you'll discover strategies for fine-tuning your money management skills and reducing costs. Singles will get pointers for successfully managing their money on their own, and families will get clear how-to information for establishing a household game plan and for encouraging family members to adopt responsible money habits. Most important, you'll learn goal-setting techniques and the simple steps it takes to reign in household spending so you'll have money left over to achieve your goals.

It's easy to spend as much or more than you earn. A few extra credit-card purchases or an emergency expense can drain the best of budgets. If debt is a concern, this book will show you the fastest way to pay down your bills.

But budgeting isn't just about paying bills. It's about viewing financial actions in a realistic light, and considering the short- and long-term costs and benefits of decisions. It's also about finding the money you need to live comfortably today while saving for the future. This book will help you avoid everyday money pitfalls and prepare for ongoing expenses and emergencies. You'll also get the worksheets you need to define and achieve your goals by building a budget that you can monitor and update for life.

How to Get the Most from This Book

This book is written to give you the practical knowledge you need to build a long-range household budget. For the maximum benefit, start with Lesson 1 and work your way through to the last chapter. Each lesson should take you about 10 minutes. This will give you the tools you need to develop a budget and the steps to take to tackle challenges you or a member of your household may have, such as binge spending, too much debt, or generally living beyond your financial means.

Conventions Used in This Book

To guide you through the lessons, the *10 Minute Guide to Household Budgeting* uses the following icons to provide useful information:

Timesaver Tip icons help you save time as you carry out the suggestions in this book.

Plain English icons define new terms.

Panic Button icons identify common problems you may confront.

What to Do Now

To get a sense of how this book works, take a look at the Contents pages to get a sense of the order in which you'll be proceeding. The *10 Minute Guide to Household Budgeting* gives you the practical advice and guidance you'll need to start controlling your financial future today.

Dedication

Dedicated to Janet Gaynor, my mom, who taught me the value of a buck and how to have fun spending it.

1

YOU AND
YOUR MONEY

In this lesson, you will learn the components of budgeting, the important role it can play in your financial life, and the tools you need to get started.

UNDERSTANDING BUDGETING

Money is like talent. Everyone has some, but a rare few have a sixth sense about using it wisely. If you're like most of us, you need a strategy for getting the most from your resources. In the case of money, the most fundamental of strategies is a budget.

In essence, a budget is a written record of the money that flows in and out of your household every month over a period of time. It provides a clear snapshot of your household income and your specific spending patterns and saving habits. It is also a precise blueprint for troubleshooting bad habits such as unnecessary overspending. By gathering pertinent household financial information into one place, a budget helps you project and plan for future expenses and goals. It also becomes a tool that takes the mystery out of your monthly cash flow and lets you control and shape your financial destiny over the short and long term.

The goal of budgeting isn't to develop an overwhelming, unrealistic document you work on for weeks, only to tuck away into a drawer and forget about because it's too cumbersome or confusing to use. By using simple worksheets that allow you, at a glance, to see where your money is going, you will be able to use your budget to stay on track every month.

Net Household Income   Your net household income is a measure of all of the money you bring in during the month, including salary, investment earnings, child support, and alimony payments, minus all deductions such as state and federal taxes and health insurance premiums.

Cash Flow   Cash flow is net household income minus bills and expenses. A budget helps you predict and monitor household cash flows.

FOLLOWING THE PAPER TRAIL

The best way to see what you spend is to write down the bills and expenses you expect to pay every month and compare them to what you actually spend in the course of each month. Then you can subtract your actual expenses from your net household income to see what disposable income you'll have after your bills are paid.

Disposable Income   The amount of income a household has left after essentials such as groceries are bought and all bills like rent or a mortgage are paid.

How much do you have left after you've paid everything to keep your household running smoothly? Where did the rest of the money go? A written budget will answer these questions and erase the guesswork many people use to manage their household finances. It will also tell you how much disposable income you can have left over to direct toward your financial goals. Lesson 3 has a worksheet and simple instructions for getting started on your own long-term budget.

Still not convinced budgeting can help you? Take a look at Table 1.1, an example of the Wilson family's budget for the month. As a preliminary exercise you too might want to try before you get out your bills, bank statements, or checkbook, the Wilsons wrote down everything they remember spending during the course of the month.

TABLE 1.1 THE WILSON'S MONTHLY EXPENSES (NET HOUSEHOLD INCOME: $2,300)

Housing	
Rent	$654
Utilities	$125
Phone	$40
Total	**$819**
Transportation	
Car payment	$225
Car insurance	$95
Gas	$35
Total	**$355**
Food	
Groceries	$325
Meals out	$250
Total	**$575**

continues

TABLE 1.1 CONTINUED

Entertainment	
Movies	$20
Video rentals	$15
Golf	$50
Total	**$85**

Personal items	
Clothing	$150
Haircuts	$35
Dry cleaning	$45
Total	**$230**

Debt	
Credit cards	$65
Personal loan	$75
Total	**$135**
Total Household Expenses:	**$2,119**

Subtract total household expenses from net household income to show monthly disposable income: $183.

WHERE DOES YOUR MONEY GO?

Do you know how much you have left over at the end of each month? Do you know how much you spend on groceries? On entertainment? In pocket money? When every purchase and bill is spelled out in black and white, you'll get precise and probably even surprising insight into your household's spending habits, where you're overspending, and where you can cut back so you can find more money to save or invest. This close-up look at your spending habits is vital as you set a plan in motion to channel your financial resources into the areas that are most important to you.

In Table 1.1, the Wilsons certainly learned a few things about their own money habits when they took a look at what they spent in the course of a month. They're trying to save for a house. That's been their goal for several years now, but there never seems to be any money left at the end of the month to tuck away toward their dream.

By writing down their actual expenses for one month, they have identified several major pitfalls in their spending patterns. For instance, they can see clearly that their habit of buying lunches in restaurants most workdays, ordering takeout dinners a few times a week, and grocery shopping without planning takes a hefty toll on their cash flow each month. They also know that they've forgotten to record some expenses because in reality they do not have $183 left over at the end of the month. In fact, sometimes they have barely enough money to cover their bills.

That's not an uncommon problem. If you can't remember where your money goes or if you feel overwhelmed by debt, Lessons 4–7 provide simple strategies to use to track where you spend your money daily, weekly, monthly, and even yearly. This will give you greater control over your finances and help you chart your future financial course, so that unlike the Wilsons, you will have something left over to direct toward your goals.

WHAT YOU'LL NEED TO GET STARTED

Here are some tools of the trade you'll need to get started on the road to solid household budgeting:

- Pencil

- Notebook (for creating budget worksheets)

- Pocket notebook (for tracking pocket money expenditures)

- Expandable file

- Checkbook register (or canceled checks) from the past year

- ATM receipts from the past year

- Credit card bills from the past year

- Calculator

Use Your Computer   If you have a computer loaded with financial planning software such as Microsoft Money or Intuit's Quicken, you can use the program to build a budget and track your household cash flow.

With a pencil, a pad, and some record of what you've spent in the last year, you're ready to begin the process of establishing a financial game plan.

In this lesson you learned the components of budgeting, the important role it can play in your financial life, and the tools you'll need to get started. In the next lesson, you'll learn how to set financial goals.

SETTING GOALS

In this lesson, you will learn how to develop a realistic list of goals and determine how much money and time it will take to attain them.

GETTING YOUR GOALS STRAIGHT

Maybe you hanker for a vacation home. Or your partner wants to go back to school. Maybe you want to invest in a mutual fund for retirement or just plain pay off debt so you have money for your hobby every month. Whatever your dream, that's the whole purpose of budgeting—getting what you want by developing a plan that lets you accomplish your goals step-by-step. Now is the time to identify what your household really wants to do with its money in the months and years ahead.

Setting specific goals and figuring out how much money and time it will take to achieve them is a fundamental part of budgeting. By committing a goal to paper and setting a timetable for achieving it, you've taken the first—and one of the most important—steps toward realizing your dream.

Visuals Help   If it's a new car you want, find a picture and post it on your bathroom mirror. Put a drawing of your dream house on the refrigerator or in your wallet, so it's a constant reminder of what you can achieve by following your budget. If you can't find a picture of your goal in a magazine, create one yourself.

WHAT'S YOUR TIMEFRAME?

Some goals are short-term and take a one- to three-year timeframe to realize. An example of a short-term goal is paying off a $1,000 credit card balance that never seems to go away. Other goals are intermediate and take approximately three to six years to achieve. For example, determining that you want to pay cash for a new car is an intermediate goal. Long-term goals that take six or more years to achieve can include buying a first home or a dream house or retiring early. It all depends on how much money your goal requires and how long it will realistically take you to save or invest that amount.

By creating a quick rendition of the worksheet shown in Table 2.1, you'll be able to keep your goals handy and determine what changes you'll need to make in your current spending habits to achieve them. For example, if your short-term goal is paying off that $1,000 credit card bill, you'll fill in the worksheet to show the overall amount you'll need to save, the monthly contribution you're able to make, and how long it will take you to save that amount.

TABLE 2.1   GOALS

My Goals	Total Amount Needed	Money I'll Save Monthly*	Time to Achieve
Short-term goals (less than 3 years):			
Pay off $1,000 card balance costing 18% in interest	$1,310	$49.50	24 months
Intermediate goals (3–6 years):			
Attend graduate school	$10,000	$130	5 years
Long-term goals (6 years and up):			
Buy a mountain cabin	$30,000	$29.50	25 years

Money you need to save monthly was calculated estimating you'll earn a 5% yield by putting your cash into a money market account every month.

 Interest Yield   The amount of interest that compounds over a specific period of time.

As you can see from the worksheet, almost any goal is within reach if you're willing to dedicate regular savings to your dream and shop for a savings or investment vehicle that pays a decent interest rate. Use a business calculator to calculate yields or have a customer service representative in your bank do it for you. As an incentive to finding a savings or investment account that pays a competitive interest rate, consider this: If you leave your savings in a non-interest bearing account, it would cost you $100 a month (instead of $29.50 a month in an account yielding 5 percent) to save for your dream cabin in the mountains over the next 25 years.

Don't forget to deduct any amounts that you might be able to shave off the total cost of a goal. For instance, if you'll be trading in a car or selling it yourself when you purchase a new one, deduct the estimated amount you'll get for the used car from the price of a new one. The same goes for homes; if you plan on selling an existing house before buying a new one, deduct the selling price.

If you already have savings earmarked for a specific goal or goals, make sure to deduct that as well from the cost of your goal. Or add an "existing savings" column, so you'll remember that you're already part way there.

GETTING THERE FROM HERE

Now it's time to record your goals. Get out your notebook and turn to the first page. Draw four columns and fill in the four category headings shown across the top of Table 2.1. Next, record the short-term, intermediate, and long-term headings on the left side of the paper, giving yourself room to record your actual goals in each category. You may first want to use a scrap piece of paper as a worksheet to help you determine what your real financial goals are and prioritize them in terms of their importance to you. As you write down your dreams on the scrap paper, try to put them in short-, intermediate, and long-term categories. For instance, a vacation you want to take to the Greek Isles in six months is more of a pressing and immediate goal than buying a vacation home for retirement. Remember to be realistic, but don't cast aside the seemingly impossible, either.

Stay After It Don't get frustrated if, to begin with, you can't save much most months. By creating and following a budget, you will have more cash to dedicate to your dreams sooner than you think.

It's not hard to get so busy with work and the daily demands of managing a household that you forget to take the time to think about what is important to your future. Goals can seem frivolous when the car needs repairs, the pet needs to go to the vet, and a pile of bills needs your immediate attention. But now is the time to figure out what goals you want to achieve to enrich your life and your household's over the next 5, 10 or even 20 years. As you control spending more carefully and pay off your debt, you'll have more cash to dedicate to your future each month.

When you've winnowed down your list to those goals or dreams that are the most meaningful to you, start recording them in your notebook. If you have to guess at how much something costs, say a new car, use a pencil to record your entry. You can obtain the precise cost later. Your goals aren't written in stone, anyway. You'll be updating your list as you achieve some of your goals and new ones become a priority.

As you determine how much money you'll need to pay or save each month and what period of time it will take you to achieve your goals, pay particular attention to those goals that are actually costing you money. If you have an overdue bill accruing late fees or a credit card or loan with a double-digit interest rate, make that kind of item a priority in terms of speedy repayment. The reason is simple: The average interest rate on credit cards has hovered around the 18 percent mark for several years now. Every $1,000 you pay off on a credit card or cash advance—which costs you 18 percent in interest to borrow—will give you (instead of your bank) an extra $180 to devote to goals each year.

Interest Rate The cost banks charge for borrowing money, or pay on accounts. Interest rates are expressed as a percentage—for example, 18%.

At the same time, don't become discouraged if a long-term
goal seems so distant it is almost unreal. Keep in mind that
time passes whether you're achieving your goals or not. It's
better to spend years to get what you really want than to never
even make the effort.

Earn Interest When You Can   Don't leave the
extra money in your budget sitting in your checking account every month. It's too tempting to
spend and you're probably not earning interest on
it. If you don't have one, open a savings account
or, at the very least, make sure you have a checking account that pays interest.

THE MONTHLY CHECKUP

Never underestimate the power of your dreams to motivate
change in your financial behavior. That's the importance of
putting your goals on paper and tracking the progress you're
making toward achieving them.

As a reminder of why you're undertaking a household financial plan, pull out your list of goals every month when you're
paying your bills and updating your budget. As you gain
greater control over problem spending areas (which Lesson 6
will help you identify), you'll be amazed at how quickly you'll
start to discover extra money every month.

In this lesson you learned how to develop a realistic set of
goals and determine how much time and money it will take to
attain them. In the next lesson, you'll start to build your annual household budget by computing your net worth.

3

CHECK YOUR
NET WORTH

*In this lesson, you will learn to compute your net worth, which will
tell you the value of what you own and how much you owe.*

HOW MUCH ARE YOU WORTH?

Your household might be in much better financial shape than
you imagined—or maybe it's a little worse off than you
thought. The only way to know for sure is to prepare a net
worth statement. By figuring our your net worth and the net
worth of a spouse or partner, you'll get a total accounting of
what you own in the way of assets and what you owe in the
way of liabilities. This will help you to see your big financial
picture and give you a tool you can use to chart the progress
your household makes each year toward paying off debt and
accumulating savings and investments.

 Net Worth   Your net worth is what you own minus
what you owe.

Assets and Liabilities   Assets are what you own, including bank accounts, investments, automobiles, jewelry, and real estate. Liabilities are what you owe, including housing payments, credit card balances, tuition, and taxes.

To fill out the worksheets starting on page 16, you'll need to pull together the following information detailing all of your and your spouse or partner's net income, assets, and liabilities:

1. Net income

   - What you earn in the course of a year from salaries, bonuses, profit sharing, investments, rental income, alimony, and child support.

2. Assets

   - *Savings.* Include the balances on any checking or savings accounts you have and cash you keep on hand. If you're unsure, check your balances with your bank.

   - *Investment accounts.* If you own any money market accounts, certificates of deposits, mutual funds, stocks, or bonds, find your most recent account statements so you'll have the values of your investments. If you've made loans to friends, family members, or business associates on which they're paying interest, include the amount you're owed.

   - *Retirement funds.* Gather your balances on any individual retirement account, annuity, pension, or retirement plan you have by looking at timely account statements or by calling your company's employee benefits department. Be sure to get a balance on any loans you've taken out against your investments.

- *Life insurance.* To find out the cash values you have in your life insurance policy and what the balances are on any loans you may have taken out, call your insurance agent. If the policies were purchased through work, call your company's employee benefits department.

- *Real estate.* If you own a home or vacation place, determine how much you owe on any existing mortgages by calling your bank or mortgage company. To find the value of your home, if you believe it has increased since you bought it, see what comparable homes are selling for by talking to neighbors or calling a real estate agent. At the same time, get balances on any outstanding home equity loan or line of credit.

- *Other assets.* If you own jewelry, recreational vehicles, artwork, collectibles, electronics, or computer equipment, estimate the value by looking in the newspaper, obtaining free appraisals, or contacting stores that can tell you the resale value of your items.

3. Liabilities

- *Loans and credit cards.* Find the balances on any personal or car loans you owe along with totals owed on any credit cards and charge cards. Make sure to include student loans and any family loans you might have. To obtain your balances, call your creditors.

- *Miscellaneous.* If you are on a revolving tuition plan, pay alimony or child support, or owe back income or property taxes, you'll need to record those amounts in this category.

CALCULATING YOUR NET WORTH

Now that you've pulled together the financial paperwork
showing what you owe and what you've accumulated in
the way of assets and investments, you're ready to begin
calculating your net worth. You can use the following
worksheet or create a similar one on paper or your computer.

Net Worth Statement for _____ Date _____

ASSETS

Cash and Investments

1.	Cash on hand	$_____
2.	Cash in checking	$_____
3.	Cash in savings	$_____
4.	Loans owed to you	$_____

Investments (estimated market value)

5.	Certificates of deposit	$_____
6.	Money market accounts	$_____
7.	Mutual funds	$_____
8.	Stocks	$_____
9.	Bonds	$_____
10.	Deferred profit-sharing	$_____
11.	Pension plan	$_____
12.	Individual retirement account	$_____
13.	Annuity	$_____

Real Estate (estimated market value)

14.	Residence	$_____
15.	Vacation home	$_____
16.	Rental property	$_____
17.	Business property	$_____

Personal Property (estimated market value)

18.	Antiques	$_____
19.	Artwork	$_____

20.	Collectibles	$_____
21.	Hobby equipment	$_____
22.	Electronics equipment	$_____
23.	Miscellaneous property	$_____
TOTAL ASSETS		$_____

Now you have a firm accounting of the value of your household's overall assets. To get a clear grasp of what you owe, list your liabilities on the following worksheet.

LIABILITIES

Short- and Long-Term Debt

1.	Charge card balances	$_____
2.	Credit card balances	$_____
3.	Personal loans	$_____
4.	Automobile loans	$_____
5.	Life insurance loans	$_____
6.	Pension plan loans	$_____
7.	Mortgages	$_____
8.	Unpaid income taxes	$_____
9.	Unpaid property taxes	$_____
10.	Unpaid service bills (attorney, accountant, medical, dental)	$_____
11.	Miscellaneous liabilities	$_____
TOTAL LIABILITIES		$_____

Deduct your total liabilities from your total assets to arrive at your net worth.

TOTAL NET WORTH	$_____

To determine what your household's annual income is, fill out the following worksheet. This gives you a clear picture of how much you have to spend as you consider what you actually spend.

INCOME STATEMENT

1. Annual salary $_____
2. Annual salary of partner $_____
3. Annual child support and alimony payments $_____
4. Bonuses $_____
5. Profit-sharing $_____
6. Dividends $_____
7. Interest $_____
8. Other income $_____

TOTAL INCOME $_____

The numbers here provide a snapshot in time of where you stand financially. Your total net worth shows you what you would have if you sold all of your assets and cashed in all of your investments, using the proceeds to pay off your liabilities. What's left over is your total net worth.

Don't be alarmed if your net worth is small or you owe more than you've accumulated in the way of assets. It's not uncommon, especially if you have a mortgage. Even if the other debt you owe is fairly high, remember that no situation is irreversible. By recording these numbers now, you have a full accounting of your current financial standing. You no longer have to guess at what your household's financial picture looks like.

WHAT IT MEANS

Your net worth statement gives you a fundamental tool for identifying problem areas, such as too much credit card debt, which you can begin to monitor and manage more closely.

You should also use the statement as a comparative bench-mark of how your savings and investment efforts are faring. Your net worth statement can also show you what impact a financial decision you are considering will have on your bottom line.

 How Much to Save   How much do you save? It's a good rule of thumb to aim toward saving 15 percent of your net monthly income. By all means, save more if you can.

Bear in mind, however, that this is not a one-time exercise. Your net worth statement will help you manage your finances on an ongoing basis by giving you an annual benchmark to use for purposes of comparison, year by year, what you earn, accumulate, and owe. For that reason, you should update your net worth statement annually, subtracting the amounts you have paid on loans, mortgages, and other liabilities. Make sure to record any new liabilities, such as a mortgage or home equity loan, as well as growth in your savings, investments, life insurance cash values, and changes in your income, on your net worth statement. This will give you a measure of the overall reduction in your debt, the growth in your assets, and a total accounting of how both impact your net worth. It should also serve as a black-and-white reminder of how far along you are toward reaching your goals.

In this lesson, you learned how to compute your net worth, providing a solid accounting of your financial health today and a reference point for your efforts in the years to come. In the next lesson, you will learn how to design a budget for the year.

4

BUDGETING FOR THE YEAR AHEAD

In this lesson, you will learn the importance of long-term budgeting in monitoring your household expenses and how to develop a budget that will serve as a financial guide for the year.

WHAT ARE YOUR EXPENSES?

There are some bills, like rent or mortgage payments, that you pay every month. Some bills you only pay four times a year, like car insurance premiums or estimated quarterly income taxes (if you're self-employed). Some bills are unplanned or come as a surprise. Maybe you have to buy wedding or anniversary presents, replace the tires on your car, or pay for emergency home repairs. Or, are you an impulse shopper or likely to jump in the car or on a plane for spur-of-the-moment vacations? Anticipating everything your household spends in the course of a year can be a challenge, but it isn't impossible if you start by first considering your fixed costs every month.

 Fixed Costs Those bills that come due regularly—say, either every month or every quarter—that require a set or similar payment.

Irregular Costs   These bills include emergency costs, such as unplanned home and car repairs, emergency medical and dental care not covered by insurance, and unplanned travel.

Building Your Budget: Step-by-Step

To begin building your year's budget, get out your notebook.

To create the worksheet on page 23, simply draw four columns on 12 pieces of paper—one for each month of the year. Make sure to leave two pages for each month—you'll need the second page later to record your emergency and discretionary spending and your savings and investments each month. By recording each of the bills you're expecting, along with the actual amounts you spend on expenses each month, you'll be able to track your spending each month and throughout the year. This will give you a detailed picture of your finances and how your household allocates its income.

Once you have that knowledge, you can begin to zero in on any areas that need your attention.

Rally Your Resources

To get a handle on how much you spend each month, pull together your household budgeting tools. They should include your budget notebook and a year's worth of bills, and whatever credit card and checking account statements or canceled checks you have. These items will tell you how much your household spent in the course of a year and exactly where the money went.

The following worksheet is just a sample for you to use as you start building your own budget. Start thinking about your fixed costs. What bills do you pay every month? If you have bills not on the list, add those items pertinent to your own expenses. It's important that you be as specific as possible when setting up expense categories. For instance, maybe you pay a large daycare or baby-sitting bill, an Internet bill, or cover some or all of a college student's or elderly parent's bills every month. Or you may have to pay your own health insurance premiums, if your employer doesn't offer health insurance or you are self-employed. If your household has a multiple number of the same type of bills, for instance two car payments, record each individually on a separate line as you build your budget.

It is also a good idea to break out credit cards and loans into their own expense categories. Of course, you'll want to ignore all of the items in the sample worksheet that do not apply to you.

Don't worry about the bills you can't remember or anticipate. The next two lessons will show you how to fill in the blanks. In Lesson 5, you'll take a closer look at what you spent over the past year to determine what irregular and emergency costs you're likely to incur each 12 months and, in Lesson 6, you'll learn to keep track of how you spend your discretionary income, the money you have left over after all of your fixed bills are paid. For now, however, focus on your fixed costs.

If you and your partner are determined to keep your finances separate, each of you can create separate budget worksheets. But if you're like most households, one person (probably you, since you're reading this book) handles most of the household's finances. Now may be the time to involve your spouse or partner, at least to the extent that you review your household's net worth and monthly budget worksheets with him or her. That helps a partner develop an understanding of your household's limitations, successes, and current financial status.

CREATING YOUR BUDGET WORKSHEET

Sample Monthly Budget			
Expense	Anticipated Cost	Actual Cost	Difference (+/–)
Rent or mortgage	————	————	————
Association fees	————	————	————
Home repairs	————	————	————
Home/yard maintenance	————	————	————
Electricity	————	————	————
Heat	————	————	————
Water	————	————	————
Sewer	————	————	————
Cable television	————	————	————
Phone service	————	————	————
Car payment	————	————	————
Gasoline	————	————	————
Commuting costs	————	————	————
Car insurance	————	————	————
Car maintenance	————	————	————
Charitable donation	————	————	————
Bank fees	————	————	————
Credit card	————	————	————
Store charge card	————	————	————
Personal loan	————	————	————
Home equity loan	————	————	————
Life ins. policy loan	————	————	————
Student loan	————	————	————
Medical bills	————	————	————

continues

continued

Sample Monthly Budget

Expense	Anticipated Cost	Actual Cost	Difference (+/−)
Dental bills	_____	_____	_____
Health insurance	_____	_____	_____
Dental insurance	_____	_____	_____
Life insurance	_____	_____	_____
Disability insurance	_____	_____	_____
Groceries	_____	_____	_____
Meals out	_____	_____	_____
Take-out meals	_____	_____	_____
Recreation	_____	_____	_____
Hobbies	_____	_____	_____
Entertainment	_____	_____	_____
Gifts	_____	_____	_____
Clothing	_____	_____	_____
Dry cleaning	_____	_____	_____
Personal maintenance	_____	_____	_____
Travel	_____	_____	_____
Magazine/newspapers	_____	_____	_____
Pocket money	_____	_____	_____

Totals

Net Monthly Income _____ _____ _____
(deduct cost totals from
monthly income to arrive
at disposable income)

Disposable Income _____ _____ _____

ANY SURPRISES?

What you have just created is one of the most important tools you can use to stay on course financially, control your spending, and achieve your goals. By using your worksheet every month, you'll forever take the guesswork out of managing your household budget. The categories show you where you're spending the most and allow you to decide where you can cut back. As several months pass, you'll see your household's financial habits begin to emerge.

Do you always go over budget in the area of groceries or meals out? Are you or a member of your household forever adding to your credit card bills, playing more golf than anticipated, or racking up ATM fees? Maybe you're one of the lucky households that spends less on certain items than budgeted. Either way, the mystery is gone. You'll be able to see what impact hitting or missing your anticipated budget has, line by line, on your overall financial picture.

In this lesson, you learned how to build a budget and record your fixed monthly costs as a measure of whether you are living within or beyond your financial means. In the next lesson, you'll see how to determine your irregular costs—those expenses we never plan for but happen just the same.

PLANNING FOR FINANCIAL SURPRISES

In this chapter, you will learn how to determine what your household's irregular costs are each year, so you can plan ahead and set money aside on a month-by-month basis to cover the inevitable.

DETERMINING THE UNEXPECTED

Irregular expenses are those bills you'll have to face in one form or another eventually, but rarely plan for. They can include repairs, taxes, and emergencies that are unforeseen, such as storm damage on a house that's not fully covered by insurance. Unfortunately, if these irregular expenses continue to fall from the sky, they can add up to play havoc with your budget.

What are some of your household's irregular expenses? Do you know what it costs you to keep your car on the road every year, or would you prefer to forget that tires go bald and brakes wear out? If you have a tendency to live month to month, without setting aside funds to cover irregular expenses, you may be putting yourself in a precarious financial position. Chances are if your car breaks down or your home air conditioning system seizes up, you'll have no way to cover the expenses except by borrowing or using a credit card. Both are expensive ways to pay for costs that should be fairly easy to anticipate.

THE PAST PREDICTS THE FUTURE

With your notebook opened to the first month's budget worksheet, take a look at the costs you weren't able to fill in previously. Now start looking through your old bills, credit card and checking account statements, or canceled checks, whichever are the most informative for telling you what irregular expenses you've forgotten about. Last year's records are about to become a road map of what you're likely to spend in the next 12 months on irregular expenses. As you find expenses, record them on a new page in your notebook so you'll be able to get a clear annual accounting of what you spend on these items. Be as specific as possible. All-encompassing categories like "repairs" or "household expenses" won't help you understand where your money goes and where you can cut back. Here's a sample worksheet that shows what the Brown family's irregular expenses amount to each year. Refer to it as you work.

TABLE 5.1   THE BROWNS' IRREGULAR EXPENSES

	LAST YEAR	THIS YEAR
House maintenance and repairs		
Gutters cleaned	$175	
Cellar leak repaired	$275	
Car maintenance and repairs		
Windshield replaced	$450	
30,000 mile tune-up	$140	
Medical and dental bills		
Root canal (portion of bill not insured)	$225	
Emergency oral surgery (portion of bill not insured)	$360	

continues

TABLE 5.1   CONTINUED

	LAST YEAR	THIS YEAR
Medical and dental bills		
Emergency room for broken toe (portion of bill not insured)	$450	
Bank costs		
Fees for ATM withdrawals	$112	
Bounced check fees ($15)	$30	
Taxes		
Tax accountant to calculate income taxes	$150	
Unbudgeted property taxes on house	$650	
Unplanned travel		
Plane tickets sick relative	$375	
Total Annual Irregular Expenses	**$3,392**	

Now that you've committed your household's irregular expenses to paper, you have an idea of how much you spend on unplanned expenses. You also have the cost information broken out into categories so you can plug it into your budget worksheet, either by filling in amounts you previously couldn't remember or by adding a new "irregular expenses" category to the worksheet.

Sometimes it can seem as if every time you turn around, you're staring down another surprise or emergency expense that requires you to borrow or use money earmarked for something else. But the type of work you're doing here will allow you to end that cycle. Now you'll be able to budget for the items by coming up with a relatively realistic projection of what such expenses will cost you in the course of a year. That allows you to plan for them on a monthly basis.

Cost Cutting Paring back or eliminating bills for those purchases or services you can either do without or provide yourself. For instance, if you pay your bank $100 a year in overdraft fees or don't maintain the required minimum balance and have to pay a monthly checking fee and per-check fees, this is an item you can cut with a little planning.

As you can see in Table 5.1, irregular expenses for this sample household came to $3,392 a year. It would cost the household $282 a month to budget for the costs ahead of time. You'll find out how much you will need to set aside each month by adding up all of your irregular and emergency expenses and dividing the sum by 12. The amount may seem painfully high when viewed as another monthly expense, but it is far easier to plan ahead than to be socked with a "surprise" tax or repair bill you have to scramble to pay. You must remember that you'll pay for irregular costs whether you budget for them or not.

Even if you do manage to pay for your irregular expenses out of pocket, it simply means that you're diverting savings you could be applying toward your goals. That may mean postponing those goals when it's not feasible to do so, such as when it comes time to replace your car.

Keep a Level Head Don't panic if you can't imagine finding the money on a monthly basis to cover your irregular expenses. Setting aside sufficient cash for such costs will get easier as you finish building your budget, begin to cut costs, and institute a regular savings plan.

Borrowing to cover the expenses, especially if you use a credit card charging double-digit interest rates, is much more painful in the long run. If you need to put necessary expenses on a credit card, it's also a sign that you're living beyond your means and you need to do some cost cutting.

BE CREATIVE

Now that you've gotten over the shock of seeing your irregular expenses laid out in black and white, look at your worksheet again, but this time with an eye toward finding unnecessary items that you can zap. For our sample household, there are several such expenses that may be optional. For instance, the family could shave $175 off its annual costs by cleaning the gutters themselves. A tax software program could save the Browns $150 in CPA charges by allowing them to prepare their own income taxes. And by doing the planning necessary to pare back ATM charges to one a week and eliminating bounced-check fees, they could save another $86 a year. That reduces their annual total for irregular expenses to $2,981 and their monthly set-aside to $248. They've just found an additional $34 a month they can put into savings or investments.

Climbing onto a ladder to clean gutters or struggling through your own tax preparation may not be a realistic option for everyone. There may be costs you've identified that you, too, cannot or choose not to eliminate. Even if you can't find items to cut from your own irregular expenses, don't despair. Planned cost cutting requires that you have a full picture of your expenses. The next two lessons will help you put the finishing touches on your budget worksheet, so you can begin cost-cutting in earnest.

In this lesson, you discovered how to estimate your household's annual irregular and forgotten costs, and how much money you must set aside each month to offset them. In the next lesson, you'll learn how to figure out what you and members of your household spend each day.

6

WHERE THE REST OF YOUR MONEY GOES

In this lesson, you will get the information you need to determine how you and your household spend pocket money every day and how to account for where your discretionary income goes.

FINDING THAT BLACK HOLE

If there still seems to be a black hole into which your money pours each month, it has to be in the area of discretionary spending. If you take money out of the bank in the morning and it mysteriously disappears from your wallet by nightfall, chances are you may not even be conscious of the spending decisions you make daily. Some people spend freely during the week. Others are weekend bingers. Some adopt a free-spending style seven days a week. But the cost of coffee drinks, meals out, take-out food, sports and entertainment events, shopping, videos, and movies can really add up. Because you probably don't get or keep receipts for all of these items, tracking them from memory can be difficult.

Luckily, there's an easier way to account for expenditures that may be taking a larger bite out of your household's budget than even necessities like housing and food do. Even if you are fairly responsible in your daily spending, you almost certainly have some expenses you'll be able to chop if you become cognizant of how much they're costing you over the course of a month or year. Other members of your household can benefit from doing the same exercise, and it may help you to soften the blow if you're planning to cut back on household allowances.

ADD IT UP

It's easier than it sounds if you actually track what you spend. Just bring a pocket-sized notepad with you wherever you go, using a page to record each day's expenditures as you make them. It's as simple as drawing three columns on each day's page. As you step up to the register for your cappuccino before work and the friendly clerk tells you, "That'll be $2.75," make a small notation in your notebook. It should include what you bought and how much you spent, and, in the third category, whether you believe the expense was necessary. When you stop by the hairdresser or barber during your lunch break, record the cost of the haircut, any hair supplies you buy, and what you tipped. The same goes for lunch, groceries after work, or take-out you pick up or have delivered. If you stop at the gas station to fill your tank, write it down. Buy a present for a family member? Write it down. You get the picture. Make sure to hand out notebooks to other members of your household whose finances are important to your budget. Make this a 30-day exercise, and you'll have a clear picture of everything your household spends in a month. Table 6.1 is an example of what a daily budget page should look like.

TABLE 6.1   **DAILY BUDGET FOR (FILL IN DATE)**

PURCHASE	COST	NECESSITY?
1. Muffin and juice	$3.50	No
2. Lunch, ice cream	$6.00	No
3. Magazine	$2.95	No
4. Dry cleaning	$17.00	Yes
5. Pizza, soda	$10.00	No
Total	**$39.45**	

At the end of the day, add up all the food, products, and services you bought. Have you actually budgeted for each item ahead of time or are you shocked at how much you spend just getting through most days? Even small items can add up to zap your discretionary income. If you have two people with free-spending habits in a household, the impact on your budget is a double whammy. But even with just one person spending freely during weekdays, the level of expenditures represented in our sample would cost a household more than $850 a month. Multiply that by 12, and you find that the sample household uses $10,200 of its income on discretionary expenses over the course of a year. That's enough cash in the course of a year to fully fund an individual retirement account, put a few thousand toward intermediate investments, contribute to short-term savings, and take a vacation.

DECIPHERING YOUR DAILY EXPENSES

What does your daily budget worksheet tell you about your own spending habits? Everyone appreciates a nice meal in a restaurant now and again. And there are items you need to purchase on a weekly basis. But budgeting is actually a strategic balancing act that requires you to choose where you want to devote your income. By keeping track, dollar by dollar, of how much you actually spend every 24 hours over the course of 30 days, you'll be able to see clearly what kind of impact your habits have on your discretionary income and make informed decisions about what lifestyle changes you'll need to make to achieve your goals.

Take a look at the spending patterns that are beginning to emerge in your daily expenses. How much do you spend on food? You'll notice our sample household spent a whopping $18.50 in one day. That's about $130 a week before groceries are even added in. We can see from just the one day's record that our budgeter has a tendency to eat out a lot. There may be other telltale indicators on the budget worksheet, too. Maybe she buys two or three magazines a week and picks up clothes from the dry cleaner four or more times a month. You'll figure out your own weaknesses after a week or two of using your daily budget worksheet. That's when the larger patterns of your spending will begin to emerge.

At the end of each week, take a page to record what you've spent overall and in each of your expense categories. Do the same for all four weeks at the end of the month. This step is key to confronting exactly how and where you're spending your disposable income. It will give meaning to the ATM and credit card receipts you stash in your wallet. The receipts can only tell you what you spend, not what you buy. You can decide where to make some of your more sweeping cuts in Lesson 7, but for now the goal is to see how much disposable income you spend over 30 days and the specific ways you spend it. Table 6.2 is a sample of what the Parson household's end-of-the-month record looks like.

TABLE 6.2   30-DAY BUDGET RECORD FOR (DATE)

PURCHASES	AMOUNT	NECESSITY?	ANNUAL COST
1. Breakfasts out	$66	No	$792
2. Lunches out	$110	Yes & no	$1,320
3. Magazines	$24	No	$288
4. Dry cleaning	$34	Yes & no	$408
5. Take-out dinners	$80	No	$906
6. Groceries	$400	Yes	$4,800
7. Clothes	$125	Yes & no	$1,500
8. Gifts	$15	Yes	$180
9. Gasoline	$60	Yes	$720
10. Haircut	$20	Yes	$240
Total	**$934**		**$11,154**

As you can see in Table 6.2, the Parsons spend a good deal of disposable income on nonessential items.

Nonessential Items   Those items that are not essential to the health or well-being of your household. Movies, meals in restaurants, and lavish clothing purchases are nonessentials. No one can go without a haircut, gasoline for their car, and groceries, but if you are attempting to squeeze money out of your budget to save or invest, some of the expenditures in Table 6.2 are avoidable. For instance, eliminating breakfasts from restaurants and coffee shops ($66), lunches ($110), and magazines ($24) on a regular basis would save this household $200 a month for a total of $2,400 a year.

As you do your own 30-day record of daily expenses, look for those nonessential items and start thinking about where you can trim. It helps to think in terms of your larger financial picture and that's what this exercise encourages you to do. That's why the fourth column with an Annual Cost heading has been added to the 30-day record. This allows you to see what different categories of daily purchases cost you over the course of the year. As you move through Lesson 7, you'll begin to make choices about spending patterns you've identified, cutting some items out of your daily budget entirely while minimizing others.

Imposing Mental Discipline

Recording your expenses gives you the chance to make specific choices about your spending, based on the knowledge of what they cost you over the course of the month. Knowing that you have to write down your purchases is an opportunity to ask yourself, before you whip out your wallet, whether you really want or need to make the purchase. Is it a necessity you're purchasing or just a typical expenditure that you're accustomed to making? As you consider the short- and long-term impact, you'll begin to see spending as a conscious decision rather than an opportunity to indulge old habits.

These kinds of choices are instrumental in curbing spending if you spend every dollar of your income every month or need additional cash to apply to debt payments or your goals.

In this lesson, you learned how to record your daily expenses so you see what you spend your discretionary income on over the course of a month and year. In the next lesson, you'll learn to determine the income you have at your disposal each week and to put limits on the pocket money you carry around and spend.

PUTTING LIMITS ON POCKET MONEY

In this lesson, you will learn how to realistically determine how much spending money you should carry and spend each week. You'll also learn how to change your banking habits and monitor pocket money on a regular basis.

DETERMINING DISCRETIONARY INCOME

Does money burn a hole in your pocket or pocketbook? Are you someone who will spend every last dollar in your wallet and then turn to your ATM or debit card for more? Worse, if you wanted something you couldn't afford, would you use your credit card?

In Lesson 6, you learned how to track and rein in your daily expenses by setting spending limits on everything you purchase from take-out food to haircuts. But sticking to a budget requires that you set aside a specific amount you can spend on discretionary items each week. Success means living by that amount regardless of what temptations cross your path. It's a matter of deducting all of your regular and irregular bills from your net income each month and deciding how you want to spend the amount left over. That amount is your disposable or discretionary income. The following worksheet provides an easy calculation for finding out how much disposable income your household has each month. Use a page in your budget notebook to keep track of your own disposable income.

Calculating Your Monthly Disposable Income

Total net income for the month $_____

minus   –

Regular monthly bills $_____

Monthly portion of variable bills $_____

Equals Disposable Income   =_____

To find out how much weekly disposable income you have, simply divide your monthly disposable income by 4. That's the amount of money you have to spend, save, and invest each week after all of your bills are paid. How you divvy up that money is up to you, but the disposable income you allow yourself each week should be written in stone. Write the amount you're allowing yourself to spend in your daily budget diary and in the back of your checkbook as a constant re-minder so you won't be able to conveniently forget you only have a few dollars left for the week when friends ask you to spend the weekend skiing or you're too tired to cook and start picking up the phone to order take-out Chinese.

UNRAVELING BAD BANKING HABITS

As you work to get spending under control, take a look at your banking habits. Here are some tips to make banking and bud-geting easier.

Ask yourself how many times a week you visit an ATM machine, use your debit card to get cash back at the grocery store, or visit a bank teller to make a withdrawal. Once a week? Five times a week? Do you keep track of those withdrawals carefully, recording each in your checking or savings register and deducting them from your balance? The simple act of banking tells you a lot about your financial habits.

Believe it or not, how often you withdraw money each week is a measure of whether or not you're controlling your spending. If your withdrawals are governed only by what needs pop up during the course of a day or a weekend, or an unplanned shopping trip regularly prompts you to whip out your checkbook, you're probably draining your disposable income unnecessarily. If you're using a credit card and not paying off your balance in full each month, the toll on your finances is worse because you're paying the card issuer interest on the money you're borrowing.

Now that you know how much disposable income is available to you each week, set a specific time each week for banking and withdraw the amount from your accounts that you've budgeted to cover your daily expenses for the week. Make banking time Monday at lunchtime or Saturday after breakfast or whichever day and whatever time works best for you. But remember, you're making a withdrawal for the week. You are withdrawing the amount you need for whatever expenses you have budgeted for, including meals out, entertainment, recreation, and even cups of coffee.

Running to the ATM in the middle of the week, when you've already made your weekly withdrawal on Saturday morning, isn't allowed unless you encounter a true emergency. Car and home repairs or a present for a friend in the hospital constitutes an emergency expense. But even then you should try to make up for the extra expenditure in the weeks that follow by trimming the amount you withdraw at banking time and adjusting your spending targets downward.

Remember to always record your ATM withdrawals and the checks you write and include a notation on what you're using the money for. Careful recordkeeping can help you in two ways: If you keep track of every withdrawal, you'll never bounce a check or overdraw your bank account, and your entries will be a constant reminder of what you're spending.

Remember, just because you have cash to spend doesn't mean you should spend it all in a day or two. You need to mete out the money you put in your wallet each payday (or ATM day) according to your needs and wants. The two—needs and wants—need to coexist. In other words, wants cannot take precedence over needs all the time. For instance, you may want a new blazer you saw in a store window, but if it's been three months since your last haircut, you probably need to visit the hair salon or barber this week. Jacket or haircut, you ask yourself. Weighing your spending decisions needs to become a conscious, conscientious task that you undertake automatically before you take out your wallet. The bottom line is, with the amount of discretionary income you give yourself as an allowance, you may not be able to both buy the jacket and get a haircut this week.

 Take a Deep Breath   If an item cries out to you and you feel yourself on the verge of buying before thinking, if it will wipe out your discretionary allowance for the week, give yourself some breathing space. Tell yourself that before making the purchase you're going to think about it overnight. Often, with a cooling-off period, you'll find that your budget-conscious self will decide that you don't need that new jacket.

HARD BUDGET MEDICINE

Of course, that kind of restraint is learned over time. It may not always work when you're just getting started on a new budget. After all, you're unlearning bad habits as you learn good ones. What happens if a bad habit prevails and by Wednesday night you've blown every cent of disposable income you've budgeted for the week? It's good to come up with a plan of action now, even before you overspend, so you'll know there are consequences to your actions when and if it happens.

What to do? Well, you have two choices. You can stick to your guns and tough it out, eating peanut butter and jelly sandwiches for two days until payday rolls around. Or, if that's not possible and you need money for transportation and food, you can borrow from what's left of your disposable income for the month. If possible, try the first option. Peanut butter and jelly never killed anyone and it's a good way to instill in yourself the lesson that your disposable income is finite. When you use it, it's really gone.

If foregoing a cash withdrawal isn't possible, borrow against the disposable income you have left for the rest of the month. But before you do, sit down with your 30-day budget record and decide where you'll make up for the borrowing. Maybe it means giving up a night of bowling or the lunch out you promised yourself the following week. It could mean diverting short-term savings you wanted to put toward a purchase into your disposable income until you make up the shortfall in the following weeks so you don't have to borrow from yourself again. However you choose to make up for the shortfall, stop the borrowing as soon as possible. It shows that your spending patterns are still not within your control, which is a dangerous sign for someone attempting to budget. You have to learn to say no—and mean it—to the worst of your spending habits.

That's especially true if you wind up withdrawing savings earmarked for other goals or, worse, using a credit card or taking a cash advance against a card to get your hands on an item you just have to have.

If such splurges become a habit, figure out what the spending triggers are so you can pinpoint your weaknesses and sidestep them.

 Trigger   A spending trigger is an event, emotion, or activity that stimulates your desire to spend money. For example, when you go to the mall, seeing all of the clothing and wares may be a trigger.

If you go shopping when your boss gets angry, head for a museum or the library instead. If you wander the mall when you're bored, find a hobby that can occupy your time without costing you money—even if it means taking a walk around the block or volunteering at a local church or YMCA. Whatever you do, stay out of the stores. Or if shopping by mail is your weakness, keep away from the catalogs.

If the call of friends who are always headed to some new restaurant or show is your downfall, learn to say no to them. By sticking to your budget now and paying attention to what such events typically cost, you'll be able to target whatever disposable income and savings you choose toward spending time and money with friends in the near future. But by then it will be a conscious decision instead of out-of-control spending.

In this lesson you learned to put limits on the way you use your household's weekly discretionary income by curbing spending and banking habits and adjusting for shortfalls. In the next lesson, you'll learn to cut the nonessential small- and big-ticket items that sap your budget over the year.

LESSON

8

CHOPPING EXPENSES

In this lesson, you will learn common-sense ways to analyze and cut nonessential items from your budget, so you'll have more cash left each month to apply to your goals.

DEVELOPING AN ACTION PLAN FOR SPENDING

Now that you've identified problem areas in your spending, it's time to take action. Your goal is to rein in expenditures that are unnecessary, but not to live the life of a hermit. At the same time, because you've already taken the mystery out of what you spend and what you want to save and invest to meet your goals, you know that unless your income is sufficient enough to meet both competing demands, you need to make adjustments. That means cutting appropriate costs in all three areas of your budget: fixed, irregular, and discretionary expenses. Hopefully, your goals are important enough to you to make those adjustments feel like a positive contribution, rather than a sacrifice.

Spending Targets   These are the goals you set for spending, to help you ensure your household isn't overspending.

Keep Using Those Worksheets   Use your actual budget worksheets to guide you as you create a new worksheet to spell out your cost-cutting targets. To develop your target worksheet, create four columns on a page. In the left column, record those expense categories you've identified as excessive in your daily and monthly budget worksheets.

TABLE 8.1   SPENDING TARGETS FOR MONTH OF _____

EXPENSES	TARGETED COST	ACTUAL COST	UNDER/OVER BUDGET
Meals out	$50	$65	+$15
Groceries	$175	$180	+$15
Phone bill	$50	$35	−$15

Seeing each month how close you come to your targeted expenses is the best way of determining whether or not you are meeting your targets.

MAKING OBVIOUS CUTS

Overspending can be caused by a variety of reasons, but bad habits usually play a central role. Those habits can range from a love of any kind of shopping to a lack of planning. The following items are the most common areas of overspending, with some commonsense solutions. If you find you overspend in different areas, you'll need to come up with your own ways to cut back.

BUDGET PROBLEM ONE: GROCERIES

Sometimes people who carefully comparison shop for weeks or even months before buying a television, a computer, or a car, pay scant attention to their buying habits in the grocery store. Putting your grocery shopping on autopilot can be dangerous, as you can see if you track how much you spend in the grocery store over the course of 30 days. Many households can wind up spending as much in a month on their grocery bill and overall food tab as they do on housing costs.

GROCERY SOLUTIONS

Plan ahead. Set aside at least one hour a week to plan your breakfast, lunch, and dinner menus and shop for the food you'll need to make all your meals at home. Make a grocery list and stick to it. Look for sales and buy only items you use. Try to steer clear of overpriced, prepackaged goods such as frozen lasagna if you can prepare the dish more economically yourself. If you notice items going bad in your refrigerator or bread box, readjust the portions you buy so you avoid such waste. Visit a warehouse food chain once a month to buy your bulk items such as paper towels, toilet paper, and detergent, but make sure you shop carefully and compare prices. Buying in bulk doesn't always guarantee you're getting a better deal, and sales at the regular grocery store may beat warehouse prices. If possible, use money-off coupons when you shop. Even if you only clip and use a few coupons a week, it will help you plan meals around economical items. Because grocery stores are becoming more competitive in trying to attract the budget-minded, make sure to join any "frequent shopper" clubs. Becoming a member usually means you'll be entitled to better savings, which may include getting deeper discount coupons in the mail, "frequent shopper" sales, or both.

 Eat, Then Shop   Be careful not to shop on an empty stomach. It will only entice you to buy items you may not need or quantities you won't be able to use.

BUDGET PROBLEM TWO: DINING OUT

Preparing meals at home takes time, not only in the kitchen but at the grocery store. There's no doubt it's easier to pick up the phone and call the pizza parlor on the corner and have dinner delivered. It's fast, it's convenient, and you don't have to think about it. The same goes for breakfast and lunch on workdays. Preparing brown-bag meals ahead of time when you're tired takes discipline if, for a few bucks, you can buy your meals at the restaurants near work. The problem is, as you've seen in Lesson 6, the cost of restaurant food can sap your discretionary income every week, every month, and even every year.

DINING OUT SOLUTIONS

View dining out, even if it's only pizza or fast food, as a luxury item you need to budget for. To ensure you don't starve at work, set a convenient but specific time each evening or morning to fix your lunch. Then remember to bring it with you. Breakfast buffs who aren't hungry first thing in the morning but habitually grab a few doughnuts or an egg sandwich on the way to work or during coffee break should make their breakfast at home at the same time they make lunch. Mid-afternoon snackers should throw some treats in the bag, too, so they're not tempted to buy bags of candy or chips when the munchies strike. If your workplace doesn't have a refrigerator, invest in an insulated lunch bag so you have a way to keep your food cold at work. If you're a big soda drinker, buy a case when your favorite brand goes on sale and take a few cans with you every day. If you're an avid coffee drinker, buy a thermos and brew an extra pot so you can have your favorite java at work.

BUDGET PROBLEM THREE: ENTERTAINMENT AND HOBBIES

Some people's budget poison may be evenings of live music, theater, art classes, or coin collecting. For others, picking up two or three videos a couple of times a week may be a mainstay of their existence. Culture is great, but too much culture, especially if it's pricey, is bad for your budget.

ENTERTAINMENT AND HOBBIES SOLUTIONS

You can still enjoy a show or a class from time to time, but you need to plan ahead. Give yourself a reason to cut back.

Maybe instead of spending $80 on two theater tickets once a month you can pare your outings to four budgeted events a year. Ask to be given tickets, classes, collectibles, or hobby equipment as presents when the holidays roll around. And make sure to take advantage of any discounts that are available. For instance, many theaters and opera houses make unsold tickets available the day of a show at heavily discounted prices. Volunteering to usher or taking a part-time job at the establishment you frequent may also net free tickets. If videos are your budget bane, set a strict limit and use any frequent renter's discounts video stores offer. If you're a hobbyist, you might be able to earn extra money by writing for a hobby group's newsletter or actively trading from your collection.

BUDGET PROBLEM FOUR: RECREATION

There's nothing like the adrenaline rush of a great run down the ski slope or a particularly fine game of golf. But both can cost $60 or more for the day (not counting the food and beverages you're bound to consume). If you're an avid athlete, you're probably also fond of the latest equipment your sport has to offer. Sports and recreational activities may make you a well-rounded individual, but you still need to be budget-minded about expenses.

RECREATION SOLUTIONS

Whether tennis or bowling is your game or you occasionally rent bikes or a rowboat as a weekend diversion, you should track the costs of these outings and plan ahead as you would for any other expense. As you decide how much you can afford to spend on recreation, try a little creativity and bargain hunting. Creativity will gain you access to favorite pastimes for free or at reduced rates. For instance, a part-time weekend job as a starter on the golf course might earn you free rounds of golf, or at least give you the earnings to pay for 18 holes. If your health or sports club is costing you a bundle, shop for a less expensive membership. Using facilities during off-peak hours or days might also provide cheaper rates. Don't forget to look for sales, either.

Sport facilities, such as ski resorts, regularly have two-for-one days that will allow you to cut your expenses in half. Sometimes, by buying a membership, you'll save overall on what you spend during a season. Or get friends and coworkers to join you on the golf course or at the gym and negotiate a less expensive group rate. If you find yourself dreaming of the latest equipment your sport has to offer or your equipment is on its last legs, budget ahead for after-season sales. The time to buy skis is not in December, nor is it wise to purchase new golf clubs in the height of summer. By targeting after-season sales, you'll also give yourself time to put the items on your goal list and to start saving now.

BUDGET PROBLEM FIVE: SHOPPING

Some people are impulse shoppers who can buy large-ticket items without blinking. Others routinely spend Saturdays roaming the mall and come home with the trunk loaded with sundry bags. If you find yourself hiding new purchases from family members because you don't want them to know you've spent yet more money, it's a good bet that you're spending too much. Whether your weakness is new clothes, computer software, or sporting goods, there are ways to avoid the heavy toll that unplanned shopping takes on discretionary income.

SHOPPING SOLUTIONS

If you're an impulse shopper, stay out of stores and away from catalogs. Don't spend rainy Saturdays in a discount mall to pass the time. If you're invited to shop-at-home parties, decline politely by telling the host or hostess you'd love to come but you're saving for a new car or whatever your goal happens to be. You need to keep temptation at bay and the best way to do that is to stay away from any situation that can persuade you to open your wallet. If you find yourself obsessing over some item that catches your eye, give yourself a specific cooling off period of at least a week (longer for expensive items). At the end of the period, ask yourself if you still want the item and can afford it. With a little luck, the temptation will have passed. If you must shop for a specific item, such as a birthday present, set a definite spending limit before you enter a store. The same goes for clothes and furniture shopping. If you know you need items over the course of the year, add an expense category to your budget for the annual amount.

BUDGET PROBLEM SIX: HOLIDAY SPENDING

You may believe that magnanimous gestures involving opulent presents are what people have come to expect from you. For some, giving extravagant gifts is a sign of wealth and generosity. For others, shopping is an ordeal they want to put an end to as quickly as possible and if that means paying a lot for a present, so be it. Either way, stores know you're a little bit desperate around the holidays and mark up items accordingly.

HOLIDAY SPENDING SOLUTIONS

Creating a list of who you need to shop for and what you've allotted yourself to spend is a critical budget tool during the holiday season. Don't leave home without your list. If you have to buy presents for a family of five, consider buying one gift everyone can use or a gift certificate for a family night at the movies, a restaurant, or even a theme park. Remember that creative, thoughtful presents, such as a basket of fruit and wine, are every bit as appreciated as pricey gifts. Giving your time in your particular area of interest or talent (whether it's computer lessons or an oil change) can also be a welcome gift. Budget ahead for special occasions and holiday presents as you would for any foreseeable expense, so you have the cash on hand instead of relying on charge cards and credit cards. Paying cash will also help you stick to your spending limits. When you start to become an old hand at budgeting, you can begin to purchase the presents you'll need for the next holiday several months, or even a year, in advance in order to take full advantage of after-holiday markdowns and other sales.

BUDGET PROBLEM SEVEN: UTILITIES

Long, luxurious showers and a bright, warm home on chilly winter evenings may be a way of life in your household. The same may apply to hours spent on the phone talking long-distance to relatives and friends. But if this kind of reach-out-and-touch everyone lifestyle is depleting your discretionary income every month, it's time to economize.

UTILITIES SOLUTIONS

Almost anyone can cut back on the utilities they use each month by applying a little discipline. Turn off lights in any room not in use. Limit showers to five minutes. Turn down heat in the winter, and put on extra sweaters and thermal underwear. Use fans and set air conditioning as high as you can without getting uncomfortable in the summer. If spring is mild or late summer brings a cold snap, turn your air conditioning unit off entirely. It may be time to start budgeting for a new air conditioner, heating system, or replacement windows for next winter. If so, add the item to your budget as a new expense category and start setting money aside every month so you'll be able to pay for the purchase out-of-pocket. Utilities companies often offer free consultations to those seeking greater energy efficiency and may offer significant discounts if you invest in a new system that is economically and environmentally friendly.

TIME TO GET SERIOUS

It's hard to give up anything that is part of your lifestyle. But if you're looking for more money to save and invest, you're going to have to make tradeoffs. That's why your spending targets are important. By putting yourself on a daily budget, you can use your spending targets worksheet to see how you fare every day over the course of a month by comparing what you budgeted for and what you actually spent. Use this, your other worksheets, and your goals as constant reminders of why you are reining in your money habits. Now that you can clearly see the long-term cost of each expense, you can ask yourself a very pointed question each time you're tempted to buy something: Would I rather have the momentary pleasure of spending money this instant or the momentous sense of accomplishment that comes from paying cash for my goal in the future?

Do the Math Translate any item you're hankering for into what it will cost you in terms of labor. If you earn $15 an hour and want a new stereo that costs $1,500, divide the cost of the item you want by your hourly wage. In this example, the math reveals you would have to work 100 hours to pay for the new stereo. That translates into two and a half weeks of full-time work for a new stereo. By attaching the value of your labor to the items you want, reining in spending should become easier.

By this time, you should also be looking at every purchase and expense as part of the whole. You know you only have so much income to go around each month. You also know that any purchase, no matter how seemingly small, adds up over the year to make a real dent in your discretionary income. Each purchase you make should be a conscious decision about how you want to use your resources. By cutting costs now so you can apply your savings to your dreams, you are controlling your financial destiny.

In this lesson you learned how to set spending limits and cut nonessential costs. In the next lesson, you will discover effective methods for getting the other members of your household to understand the benefits of budgeting and apply some of the techniques you've learned so far.

9

GETTING YOUR HOUSEHOLD TO BUY IN

In this lesson, you will learn how to get the members of your household to cooperate with your budget efforts. You'll also learn how to help them set goals and spending targets they can live with.

EDUCATING YOUR FAMILY

Now you're armed with the tools to effectively manage your household budget and make informed spending decisions. But are the other members of your household in full accord? If you have a family, they should know about your efforts. Trying to institute and manage a budget without household members' cooperation is like having two people in a boat rowing in opposite directions—you won't get very far. It's important for all members of a household to play a role in budgeting. Everyone involved should understand the benefits that will be reaped by conscientious money management and the damage that can be done by poor money management.

Chances are you're excited about the prospects of being able to control your financial future, whether it means digging your way out of debt to make a fresh start, accelerating savings for retirement, or just buying a new computer. But a spouse, partner, or kids may have other pressing matters at the top of their priority list. Don't be disappointed if they are initially reluctant to join you wholeheartedly. The best way to show anyone the merits of your efforts is to get them involved from the beginning. Maybe that isn't possible. Perhaps you don't want to show your kids your finances, or you have a spouse or partner who doesn't have the time or interest. You may be the designated bill payer and money manager. In any event, even if you're the point person for creating and managing your household's budget, you will still need other members' cooperation. Careful budgeting requires a lifestyle change for everyone involved. It's a family affair and because you're becoming the knowledgeable budget expert, you have to lead the way.

START WITH GOALS

Instead of zeroing in on your family's bad habits, show them the benefits of budgeting first. Maybe a spouse has been hankering for a new car or your entire family wants to take a trip across the country. Show them how long it will take to achieve this goal and how much must be set aside each month using the table in Lesson 2. It's important they understand that it will take a specific amount of time and money to achieve this goal. It's equally important that they understand that using a credit card to make a purchase is not an option. The goal of careful budgeting is to find more money within the income of your family to reach your goals. Using a credit card and paying interest charges defeats the purpose of long-range planning.

With a little luck your goals are shared ones, so you don't have to bicker about where your money will go once you've saved it. If they're not, compromise. If a spouse or partner wants a vacation home and you want to increase retirement savings, devote money to each goal. It's crucial that all members of your household have some input into the family's goals or they'll have no reason to follow a budget.

You may want to allow children to set their own reasonable goals so they can begin to appreciate managing their finances and saving on their own. Help them create a version of the goal worksheet in Lesson 2. Maybe they want new a new computer program or bike. By giving them their own goal worksheet, it becomes easier for you to say no when they ask for something that is not an immediate necessity. Instead of a fight, tell them to put the new item on their goal worksheet, figure out how much it costs, and how long it will take to save for the item. You can always compromise, if you care to, by offering to match some or all of what they save for a specific item. In any event, this exercise helps them to appreciate the value of money and that sometimes they have to be willing to work and save for the things they want. Who knows, you may get them started on saving for a car, college, or even interested in putting money into an IRA.

tip

Make It Visual   Whether you're attempting to help a spouse, partner, child, or elderly parent become more budget-minded, visuals can help them keep their goals in mind, just as they help you. Urge them to find a picture or photo of the image that best represents what they want to use their money for and put it in a prominent place as a reminder that budgeting will help them achieve their dreams.

TAKE A LOOK AT SPENDING HABITS

Once you have the members of your household sold on shared and individual goals, you can ease them into the changes in lifestyle and spending necessary to make these goals possible. Explain up front that budgeting means harnessing more income to use the way your household wants to use it, rather than playing catch-up on bills. That means everyone will have to make some sacrifices. No one can have everything they want when they want it.

So that they fully understand how much they are spending and how these spending habits get in the way of their goals, it may be necessary that they keep track of everything they spend daily in a pocket-sized budget notebook of their own. If that's not possible, create a daily budget worksheet to keep on the refrigerator door and gently remind them at the end of the day to fill in what they've spent on food, recreation, gas, and anything else they've bought.

You can turn this into a meaningful game for the kids in your household by helping them remember what they've spent during the day on school lunches, treats, and other items. Ask them if the money you give them for allowance or the cash they earn working could be put to better use. If they continue to spend the way they do, will their financial situation improve, stay the same, or worsen? What can they change in their spending habits to make it easier for them to afford their goals? As they keep track of their daily expenses, they, too, will come to realize that every decision to spend money has a consequence. Spending money is a choice. They can spend it quickly now or save for more important goals. They can't do both.

Now that members of your household can see for themselves what their spending actually costs, they should have a clear sense that their finances are within their control and their goals within their grasp. The mystery that often surrounds money should be gone. If kids get an allowance every week, they now know where it goes and how they could be using it. Their clearer understanding of the necessity of budgeting should make it easier to justify some of the other changes you will need to make.

If they're interested in starting a savings plan, help them set up one at the bank. The same goes for a spouse or partner, for whom savings may be new.

INFLICTING PAINLESS LIFESTYLE CHANGES

Once you've agreed on the importance of specific goals, it's time to start discussing the types of spending changes that will allow your household to cut costs and make meaningful contributions to savings. You've already seen what larger household expenses cost your family, what daily expenditures cost, and identified ways to trim back or eliminate those expenses. Again, however, you need your family's help.

Don't spring surprises on them by turning off the heat or coming home from the grocery store with a side of beef and no snacks. Set some time aside to discuss as a household where the biggest budget traps are and how and where you can change or eliminate those expenses. It might mean the kids have to help out with lawn care or cut back on renting videos. Maybe instead of giving them lunch money every day, you want them to take their lunch to school. The same might apply to your spouse.

Sometimes lack of communication and an action plan can be the biggest impediments to successful family budgeting. Putting a ban on take-out food orders and telling your family you want them to take their lunches instead of buying them may not work if there aren't enough groceries in the refrigerator for the week. You have to make sure your household has the resources and initiative it needs to carry through with a budget plan. To get the ball rolling, sometimes more drastic action is necessary. You may want to allocate chores (grocery shopping, dinner, brown-bag lunch preparation), using an assignment list for each task. If it's easier for you to take care of meals yourself, so be it.

In any event, make sure that all of your household's spending cuts and targets are fully understood by each member of your family. That goes for larger items, too, such as clothing allowances. By setting a target amount for the year that incorporates back-to-school clothes and seasonal needs, you should be able to avoid conflicts. By having a specific amount of money to spend, members of your household have the ability to make choices and to see the consequences of them. Planning shopping excursions ahead of time with spending limits in mind is a good way to communicate both the maximum dollar amount available and the need to make choices.

If you've budgeted $350 for your 13-year-old's return to school, let him or her know that it's the maximum amount he or she can spend on shoes, a winter coat, and any other clothing they might need until spring. If they set their heart on a leather coat that will eat up every penny in their fall-winter clothing budget, make sure they realize that the coat should be important enough to them that they're willing to do without another item until their birthday or a holiday rolls around. Try to be reasonable, but firm. No one ever died because they couldn't buy their fifth pair of jeans or third pair of running shoes. Limits might also force them to be more creative—an area in which you can encourage them. It may, in fact, be time for a baby-sitting or weekend job that will finance the items they desire. Or maybe they can shop second-hand stores for that classic leather bomber jacket so they'll still have money left for a few sweaters and a new pair of jeans.

Overall, involving kids in household budget exercises should help them realize the value of a dollar, a valuable lesson for them to take with them into adulthood.

BUDGETING BY EXAMPLE

As you begin to attack other expenses, such as large hot-water bills, you have to walk the walk, too. If you set a five-minute limit on showers, that means five minutes for everyone, including you. Putting a clock in the bathroom should serve as a reminder of the need to be quick. Let family members know that they need to turn off the light when they leave a room. Prepare them for the onslaught of winter—if they intend to turn heat down—and coming of summer—if you plan to use the air conditioning less.

You might also want to consider setting limits on long-distance phone calls or asking kids to pay for their calls themselves. As an added reminder that time is money when you're on the phone, put a small clock and phone log by the phone and ask each member of your family to sign in at the beginning of their calls, recording who they're calling and what time the call starts and ends. At the very least, make sure you show them the phone bill monthly so they know how much individual calls cost. Record your own long-distance calls, too.

If an overabundance of video rentals is a problem, you can also set limits here. Instead of allowing family members to rent five videos, limit video selections to one a weekend. If late return fees are a running battle, designate a person whose job it is to return the video before it's late.

Make sure to communicate the ways in which you are limiting your own spending and the lifestyle changes you are making. Tell them when you're passing up a fancy meal and cooking at home instead. Let them know when you've decided to forego an expenditure for one more season, so you can put the money in savings instead. Being up front about your own good money habits and the new sense of control you feel over your finances should make the transition to good budgeting easier for the other members of your household.

SHARE THE RESULTS

As the results of your household's new budget begin to roll in, let everyone know. If it's bad news, such as a large long-distance phone bill, discuss it and ask what went wrong. Solicit suggestions on ways to prevent the same problem from cropping up next month. If the results are good and your family has hit or underspent spending targets, share that news, too. Whether you've spent less on videos, after-school treats, or recreation, let your family see your budget worksheet from month-to-month, so they can see for themselves the fruits of their budgeting labor. If possible, show them where the saved money is going, whether it's toward bills or into a savings or investment account. Remind everyone, including yourself, that you've just taken another step closer to your goals and that budgeting really does work. Kids, in particular, need constant reinforcement.

No one unaccustomed to saving becomes an instant budget success. Entire households whose members have differing priorities and agendas can take a long time to get the hang of things. But if as a result of your efforts your family members think before they buy, cut costs where they can, and realize that achieving goals requires them to take responsibility on a daily basis for spending and saving, you've won 90% of the battle. Winning the rest may take time and gentle, but constant, vigilance on your part. As time rolls by, you'll start to achieve the type of financial success that should encourage everyone in your family to get their budgeting act together.

DEALING WITH THE UNCOOPERATIVE

You may have a household member who, for whatever reason, does not share your enthusiasm for budgeting or see it as a top priority. If showing by example, cajoling, and setting limits doesn't work, you need to minimize the damage they can do.

If a spouse or partner doesn't want to cooperate, you may need to obtain separate checking and savings accounts, so you retain the ability to manage your own income. If debt is a problem, cancel credit cards. Even if a partner is less enthusiastic than you are about budgeting, make sure to share the news of your successes, such as smaller bills, larger savings, and new investments. Make sure to remind them that you're ready to help them put their money to better use whenever they have the time. Small efforts, such as making their lunch or washing shirts they usually get dry-cleaned, might also encourage them to take the first few steps toward living by a sane budget.

Kids are another matter. They may have a difficult time grasping why they can't have a new bike so Mom and Dad can save for retirement. But chances are good that because you're the adult, you have the upper hand. If after you've honestly communicated your goals and the spending cuts you intend to make, and they still won't cooperate, consider more drastic actions. If pricey long-distance calls continue to be a problem, put a lock on the phone. If they still rent videos on your account without paying for them, hide the VCR or cancel the account. If they return the family car without refueling, put a moratorium on its use. They may not believe you when you tell them it's for the good of your family, but at least you'll have tried.

In this lesson, you learned how to get your family on board with your budget plans. The next lesson is for singles who need added help to curb spending and change their outlook on money.

SINGLE AND SAVVY

In this lesson, those of you who are single will learn to take tougher measures to curb spending and start making headway with your budget.

STRATEGIES FOR CUTBACKS

If you're single, you don't have to face an angry partner when you make financial mistakes. If no one blows up at you when you waste the grocery money on a new suit, allow unpaid credit card bills to pile up, and still live the high life, it doesn't mean you've gotten away with anything. When it comes to budgeting for the future, there is no free lunch. That's particularly true of singles, who tend to earn less and spend more when compared to their married counterparts. It's true that having no one but yourself to answer to can make you financially footloose and fancy free. You're prone to a different lifestyle than couples and may be more prone to temptation from friends who dine out, shop often, and travel extensively. Although these activities can be more fun than reading a book, blowing every last cent and then some on a spendthrift lifestyle may lead you to postpone important financial decisions indefinitely. The longer you postpone saving and investing, the harder it becomes to play catch-up. Yet the necessity of saving and investing is particularly keen for singles because they do not have the financial safety net of a spouse. Luckily, there are some simple strategies that can help you overcome bad habits and get on a realistic budget track.

Become Your Own Budget Boss

Sometimes committing a budget to paper just isn't enough to change your habits. Perhaps you need to take a hard and fast look at why and when you spend. If you're planning a quiet (and inexpensive) evening at home and friends call from the neighborhood pub, do you jump in the car? Are you packed and out the door when someone invites you skiing or to the beach, before you even consider what the trip will cost or whether you can afford it? Is meeting friends or co-workers at different restaurants for lunch a daily habit? You need to figure out your own spending triggers so you can learn to say no, at least some of the time.

Planning Saves Money   If you find yourself facing Friday without a concrete plan for the weekend, you'll be more vulnerable. Get out your calendar and the weekend section of the newspaper and figure out what inexpensive or free fun can be had right in your backyard. Try to plan a month's worth of activities. Visit museums, go to the library for a free lecture, walk around a festival, or take a picnic lunch to a park you haven't visited before. Invite your friends to come along. To keep your social calendar chugging along, initiate a once-a-month book club, a volleyball game, or a card game.

If bringing your lunch to work is hard because everyone goes to restaurants and you don't want eat alone, start a lunch club and have everyone take turns bringing lunch for others at least one day a week. Order take-out pizza or other inexpensive meals you can all chip in for. You can also suggest eating establishments with settings that allow you to bring your lunch, such as the local mall's food court or the office cafeteria. There may be days when you find yourself eating alone at your desk or in the park. Take a walk around the block, read a book, or, better yet, look over your daily and monthly budget worksheets. This will show you the positive effect your efforts are having on your bottom line.

If restaurants are a financial stumbling block for you at night but a frequent pastime for friends, find ways to eat your dinner at home and join friends later for dessert or coffee. Creativity can go a long way toward helping you find your own budgetary comfort zone and still spend time with friends. You will also want to make meal planning and grocery shopping a regular part of your weekly schedule so you won't be able to use the lack of food as an excuse to eat out or order in.

Remember that there will be times when you have to say no to invitations and urges to spend. Whether you tell friends you're cutting back or not is up to you. The important thing is not to sabotage yourself. Spending a Saturday at an outlet mall and hoping you won't buy anything may not be realistic if you know shopping is a weakness. Don't put yourself in situations where it is easy to fail.

Being your own budget boss means you don't have to compare yourself to couples or individuals who seem to have more money than you. Budgeting isn't about earning more money. Some people will spend every dime they have, no matter what they earn. Budgeting is about keeping more of the money you do earn. That means living within your means and controlling how you use your discretionary income.

DON'T BE OVERZEALOUS

Maybe you gave budgeting a try and it didn't work before because you chopped too deep, paring every pleasant activity and expense from your monthly routine. It's unrealistic to expect much success if you make budgeting a misery. You have to decide what you can live without and what you can't live without. If restaurant lunches are a priority, find something else in your budget to chop. Or take your lunch to work Monday through Thursday and treat yourself to lunch out on Fridays. Maybe you're willing to give up lunches if you can use some of the money for an occasional weekend trip or sporting event. What's important is planning the costs in advance and writing down and sticking to your spending limits.

Budgeting really is a game of tradeoffs. You don't have to give up everything all at once or forever. The trick is to identify those expenses that really sap your discretionary income every month. By looking at your regular and irregular expenses and keeping a daily financial diary, you know what your out-of-control expenses are. Start your cost-cutting efforts slowly by zeroing in on the one or two items that cost you the most each month. You'll have a better chance at sustained success.

DO YOUR HOMEWORK

If your spending habits are hard to break, make sure to keep up your financial diary every day. Record all those expenses you incur from morning until night. It will give you important insight into which habits you're controlling and which are still getting the best of you. This will give you the tools you need to put the brakes on problem spending areas. As another reminder of whether or not you're living within your budget, keep a copy of your spending targets from Lesson 8 in your diary. You'll be able to use those targets every week for check-ups of whether or not you are controlling your expenses. The target worksheet will tell you how much out-of-control spending is costing you. It will also be the best indicator of your cost-cutting successes, which are certainly worth looking at regularly.

You may also want to add your goals worksheet to your financial diary, so you'll remember why you're at your desk during lunch or skipping a Friday night foray to the local pub. If you need to, look at the pictures of your goals every day to remind yourself why you're making changes in your financial life. If your first goal is a vacation, imagine yourself in your locale of choice every time you're tempted to buy something. Instead of feeling deprived, you should feel a sense of pride in the fact that you're taking control of your finances and will be able to reap the short- and long-term rewards. You'll be your own financial boss, which is a necessity because there are no other bosses in your household.

IF YOU FAIL, START AGAIN

If you fall off the budget wagon, don't give up. If you're living exactly as you lived before you began budgeting (for example, no groceries, no activities planning, no cost-cutting), it's no wonder you're not making any headway. You're still putting yourself in harm's way. It will be almost impossible for you to succeed in saving and investing more for your goals until you put yourself in control of your money. That means you'll have to change at least some of your money habits and make each expense a conscious decision before—not after—the sales clerk has rung up a purchase. Luckily, it's never too late to start budgeting again. When you overspend or buy items you haven't planned for, figure out what went wrong and how you can avoid making the same mistake again. Then start fresh the next day. If possible, repair the budget damage as soon as possible by cutting back on other expenses. Remember, while there is no one there watching you stumble or succeed financially, there may be no one there to help you out if you fail, so it's particularly important as a single person to get your financial house in order.

In this lesson, you learned ways to minimize some of the budgetary pitfalls that plague singles. In the next lesson, you'll learn how to evaluate the cost of the debt you have and to avoid using credit in the future while reducing the debt you have now.

TACKLING YOUR DEBT

In this lesson, you'll learn to how to evaluate the cost of the debt you have and learn ways to avoid using credit in the future while reducing the debt you have now.

HOW YOU USE CREDIT

If you're a fan of credit cards or loans, you probably know how easily small purchases can add up to sizable balances and unwieldy monthly payments. Charge a vacation, an emergency car repair, a few restaurant tabs, and add to your wardrobe on your credit card while using the handy loan checks your bank sends you around the holidays to buy gifts and you're probably looking at some serious debt. That debt is only compounded if you've experienced a bout of unemployment or some serious medical emergency that wasn't fully covered by insurance. As you know better than anyone, if you have a car payment, a mortgage, or even sizable student loans on top of that, you're treading dangerous financial waters and may only barely be keeping your head above water every month when the bills come due.

It's not a very comfortable way to live. That's probably why you've made finding your way back to the safety of a sound financial footing a priority. No matter how unwieldy your debt is now, paying it off is less difficult than you think if you're determined to reform the way you spend money.

LOOK AT YOUR HABITS

First, it's important to understand how you got into trouble in the first place. If you incurred your debt during a time of emergency, say because of an illness or car accident that kept you out of work, and you were forced to take out credit card advances (an unwise though not uncommon activity for people facing a financial shortfall, by the way), your best hedge for the future is to follow the plan laid out in Lesson 12. It will show you how to accumulate enough savings to cushion your budget from future high-interest rate borrowings in the future.

At the opposite end of the spectrum is the free spender. Who qualifies as a free spender? Someone who spends money they don't have (not once, but repeatedly) and on items they don't need. A free spender is someone whose motto is: "Have plastic, will purchase." Maybe you use checks or stop by the ATM machine before shopping sprees, but the result is the same.

If you're living beyond your means every month, buying goods, services, and entertainment you can't afford but think you deserve anyway, you're going to have to apply the spending brakes. A good way to get started is to revisit Lesson 6 and start using a pocket-sized notebook to record each and every expenditure you make every day. After 30 days, compare your notebook with your monthly budget worksheet to see how far you've exceeded your spending targets and in what areas. Seeing what you actually spend and being able to compare it to what you actually should be spending will show you where your problem areas are. Now it's time to take some positive action.

An Action Plan Against Future Debt

Before you tackle a payment plan, remove yourself from harm's way. The best way to ensure you don't spend freely again tomorrow or when the weekend rolls around is to get rid of all temptation. That means removing all of your credit cards, store charge cards, ATM cards, and checks from your wallet and putting them in a drawer. Before you do that though, write the balance you owe on each on a small piece of paper and tape it to the appropriate instrument. If you owe money on overdraft protection, tape the balance to your ATM card. Bank loan balances should be taped to your checkbook, and so on. Then put the lot of them in the drawer. Take out what you need only when you visit the bank to get the cash you've budgeted for the week. Then put your checkbook or ATM card back in the drawer.

If, for whatever reason, putting your spending tools in a drawer doesn't do the trick, cut up your credit and charge cards. You can ask the bank or stores for duplicates later when you pay off the balances. If you're still visiting your drawer to nab your ATM card and using the corner ATM machine at the drop of a hat, you may have to cut that up, too. Forcing yourself to visit a bank branch to make a withdrawal with a withdrawal slip is less convenient and may give you the financial resolve you need to stop overspending.

If you've kept track of your spending habits for 30 days, you've identified your weaknesses and now is the time to design your own "stay out of trouble" strategy. Accomplishing that will mean staying away from all the places that tempt you to make unbudgeted expenditures. If the mall is a prime recipient of your credit cards, stay away from stores for 30 days. If nightclubs or restaurants get the majority of your cash and then some, steer clear of them for the month. If unplanned weekend outings are the prime cause of your debt, make them taboo for 30 days. Learn to say no to any person, place, or event that has caused you to open your wallet to unplanned expenses in the past or scrub them from your routine during your "stay out of trouble" month.

After the 30 days is up, look at the new bills you get in the mail. You should be pleasantly surprised. Because you didn't borrow or charge during the month, you'll notice there are no new purchases on your credit and charge card statements. You'll also notice that your payments actually made a dent, however small, in what you owe, provided you're not being charged more in interest than what you paid.

Even if your payments didn't reduce some of your debt, you've plugged the dam by avoiding all unnecessary expenditures for the month. You've taken control of your spending. Now, extend your "stay out of trouble" strategy for another month and prepare for a dose of reality regarding what your past free-spending lifestyle is *really* costing you.

THE ULTIMATE PRICE YOU PAY

Making a dent in your overall debt can be a problem, especially if your balances and the interest rate you're being charged are unwieldy and you're only paying the minimum payment your creditors request each month. If they had their way, you'd take years to pay off your charge cards, credit cards, and loans. But you don't want to do that. Here's why: The average credit card charges you interest rates that are just over the 18% mark, so unless you pay off your balances in full each month, you're being charged a bundle for the privilege of using credit. The typical credit card balance in the United States hovers around the $2,500 mark. If you carry that balance for a year and you're paying 18% in interest, you're coughing up $450 in interest alone over the course of 12 months. A $5,000 balance at 18% costs you $900 in interest rate charges, a $7,500 balance $1,350, and a $10,000 balance costs you $1,800 a year. If you're someone who is still paying off Christmas or holiday presents from 1993, can you calculate what those presents actually cost you?

If, instead, you were able to invest the interest charges (not your actual debt payments, mind you, just the interest you're being charged) you pay every year, over time you could finance a college education and a secure retirement. You might even be able to retire early.

What You're Missing Out On

Money spent on debt payments is money you're not putting to work for you. If you're heavily into debt, you may be making your bank rich and the shareholders of the stores you frequent extremely happy, but consider the overall costs to your own financial plan and dreams. The fact is, you're paying even more than the interest you're being charged. Why? Because money spent on debt is money that isn't invested. If the cash isn't working for you, you're losing out on the interest you could be earning.

To see how much you're really losing, take your monthly debt bills for the year (excluding, to be fair, your mortgage if you have one) and imagine that you've put the money instead into a stock market mutual fund where, based on historical returns over the past 20 years, you can expect a 10% return annually. What would your "investment" be worth after a year? After two years? If your debt payments are $300 a month, you'd accumulate a $3,960 nest egg after only one year. In two years, you'd have $8,316. It's something to think about the next time you whip out your credit card or store charge card or are tempted by the handy convenience checks that banks and credit card companies have a way of sending spenders, especially around the holidays. Seeing what you could be earning with your money, instead of sending your hard-earned cash to your bank and other creditors each month, should be an incentive to pay down your debt as fast as possible.

Building a Payment Plan That Works

Regardless of the size of your debts, there are two prime components to any successful debt repayment plan: Pay as much as you can as often as you can. The more you pay, the less you'll owe in interest charges and the more you'll be able to dedicate to other bills, until all of your debt is paid off and you can apply your money to your savings and investments.

By keeping a worksheet, you'll be able to graphically illustrate how much you owe on each debt, how much you've paid, and what your balance is each month. It's also a handy way to track the interest you're being charged along with any late fees you've accrued. Here's what the Smith household's debt planner looks like for three months.

 Revolving Debt   Revolving debt is any bill you cannot pay off each month. Revolving debt includes credit card and store charge card balances, car, home equity, and student loans as well as medical, dental, legal, and tax bills.

THE SMITHS' DEBT PLANNER

Credit Company	Loans		Credit Cards			Other Revolving Debt	
Starting Date	Auto 2/94	Personal 1/96	ABC card 10/95	DEF card 12/96	XYZ card 5/97	Dentist bill 2/95	Hospital 6/96
Total Owed	$1,400	$2,200	$2,200	$900		$50	$450
Interest Rate	13%	17%	18%	16.5%	5.9%	10%	15%
January							
Amount Paid	$175	$65	$35	$15		$25	$25
Interest	$15.16	$31.16	$33	$12.37		.41	$5.62
Late Fee	$15	$15					
Balance	$1,255.16	$2,181.16	$2,198	$897.37		$25.41	$430.62
February							
Amount Paid	$160	$65	$45	$20		$25.62	$25
Interest	$13.59	$30.89	$32.97	$12.33		.21	$5.38
Late Fee							
Balance	$1,108.75	$2,147.05	$2,185.97	$889.70		$0	$411
		Transfer balances on both cards to low-rate XYZ card					
March							
Amount Paid	$160	$90			$65		$25
Interest	$12.01	$30.41			$15.14		$5.13
Late Fee							
Balance	$960.76	$2,087.46	$0		$3,025.81		$391.13
Total	$960.76	$2,087.46	$0	$3,025.81	$0		$391.13

As you can see, the Smiths are carrying a heavy debt load. They paid $375 in debt payments the first month they embarked on their new debt management plan. They were also the victim of their old habit of making late payments and got hit with $30 in late fees their first month—a habit they changed by writing due dates in red on a big calendar they keep in their kitchen.

But by tracking their debt in writing, several things quickly became crystal clear to the Smiths. For instance, they saw that by making the minimum payments on their ABC and DEF cards each month—which barely covered the interest they were being charged—it would take them years to pay off their original balances. So they increased their payments slightly. They also recognized that the interest rates (18% and 16.5%, respectively) they were being charged on both of their credit cards were not as competitive as they should be. So they applied for and got a new card from XYZ bank, which offered them a 5.9% interest rate. Then they transferred both their credit card balances to the new card and saved $29.87 in one month. They were unable to refinance their personal loan with its hefty 17% interest rate, so when they finished paying off their dentist bill in February, they applied that $25 payment to the $65 they had been making on the loan. That makes sense, because they're paying the highest interest rate on that loan. In October when they finish paying off their auto loan, they'll apply that $160 payment to their personal loan as well.

Their strategy is paying off in two ways. First, they've decreased their overall debt payments each month from $375 to $340, just by switching their credit card balances to a card that charges less interest. Second, as they finish paying off a debt, they apply the payment to the debt charging them the highest interest rate. If they stay on track, they'll finish paying off their personal loan in March of next year and can apply that payment to their credit card. Within two years of embarking on their debt repayment plan, the Smiths will be completely debt free.

Two years may seem like a long time to pay off debt, but it probably took years to accumulate the burden you're carrying right now. It's only logical that repayment will require patience and discipline. All good things worth having are worth planning for. Instead of concentrating on how long it will take you to free yourself of your creditors, think of the rewards. In two years, the Smiths will be able use the $340 they were paying to creditors each month any way they choose. If they save the money in a checking or money market account that pays 5% in interest, they'll have $4,320 after a year.

MAKING DEBT LESS BURDENSOME

As you start your own plan, here are some of the actions you can take to ensure that repayment is as easy and quick as possible:

- *Avoid late payments.* Paying your bills late each month can cost you hundreds of dollars extra each year. That's money you should be using to reduce your debt. If you make late payments frequently, try posting a big calendar in the room you do your bills in each month, then write the due dates prominently on the calendar in bold ink. Many banks offer a free computer bill payment program that allows you to designate that bills be paid electronically on a certain day each month. You can set the program on auto-pilot if you wish by requesting that payments be made to certain creditors automatically each month, whether you log on to the program or not. If you have a computer and a modem, using a computer bill-payment program is an excellent way to avoid late payments. Some banks also offer a phone bill-payment program at a minimal monthly charge that allows you to set up regular bill payment by phone.

- *Don't pay the minimum.* Paying only the minimum your credit card company requires you to pay each month almost guarantees that it will take you years to pay off a single balance. You must pay more than you're being charged each month in interest to make a dent in the balance you owe. Even if you can only afford to pay $10 or $20 extra each month, you'll hasten the time it takes you to close out balance.

- *Trade in your expensive balances.* If the rates charged by your credit cards issuers are higher than 6%–10%, it's time to embark on a two-part strategy to lower your interest rates. First, look for a low-rate card offer in the mail or even get the name of a bank offering a good deal from a friend. Then call up your credit card company and tell them you want them to match the rate you've been offered or you'll transfer your balance to the lower rate card. If they consider you a good customer, they'll probably give you their lowest introductory rate. If they don't, apply for a low-rate card and consolidate all of your card balances on the new low-rate card. As you saw in the previous table outlining the Smith's debt planner, transferring balances to a card with a more competitive rate can shave hundreds off your interest tab each year and give you more money to apply to your actual debt.

- *Watch for expiring low-introductory rates.* Some credit card issuers only keep the interest rates they offer on a new card low for three to six months, then it jumps to 17% or more. If the expiration date for a low rate isn't clear on an offer, call the credit card company's toll-free number and ask how long the low rate will last. Shop for a rate that is guaranteed to stay low for six to twelve months and mark your calendar a month or so before expiration so you'll have time to shop for another low rate if you need to.

- *Use found money.* If you get a raise or bonus at work or an income tax return you can spare, apply the extra money to your debts. The lower your balances, the lower the interest rate charges you'll be assessed and the quicker you'll pay off those balances.

- *Make smart payments.* As you pay off one debt, apply that amount to your other debts charging you the highest interest rates. Continue that practice until you're debt-free.

- *Consider consolidation.* If your personal loans cost you 14% or more in interest charges each month, shop at banks and credit unions in your area for a lower-rate loan. If you find one, apply and use the proceeds of the loan to pay off your other loans. This will give you one less-expensive loan payment each month and save interest charges.

- *Pare student loans.* If the total of your student loan payments is unwieldy and you need a lower payment, you have several options. You can seek out a consolidation plan from your bank or from the Student Loan Marketing Association (Sallie Mae). All are required to offer a variety of consolidation programs, which include either initial low payments or extend the life of the loan. While giving you cheaper monthly payments, at least initially, consolidating all of your student loans guarantees that you'll pay more in the long run.

  If Sallie Mae has bought your loans, you can save without consolidation. If you pay on time for 48 months, Sallie Mae shaves your interest rate by two points. If you allow the corporation to debit your checking account for payment each month, they'll rebate all but $250 of your loan origination fees.

- *Refinance your mortgage.* To see if refinancing your mortgage makes sense, find the best combination of low interest rate and closing costs, including points (a point is 1% of your loan amount) and then do the following math. Divide your closing costs by your monthly savings on the mortgage payment the new loan will give you. What you'll get is the break-even point or the number of months it will take you to pay off your closing costs before your loan is actually cheaper. If you plan to stay in the house significantly longer, refinancing will save you money in terms of your monthly mortgage payment. Remember, however, that a lower rate means you'll have a smaller income tax deduction for mortgage interest. If you have questions, get a mortgage banker to run your numbers and explain any savings you can realize by refinancing your mortgage.

After you finish paying off all or most of your other debts, you also might want to consider applying some of those debt payments to your mortgage. By applying extra cash to your mortgage every year, you can shave up to a decade or more off a 30-year loan. To turn a 30-year, $100,000 mortgage into a 20-year mortgage will cost you $175.99 extra a month. Everything you pay above and beyond the monthly mortgage payment the bank requires you to pay reduces the principal of your loan and shaves years and interest charges off your overall mortgage.

READY FOR REPAYMENT

Now that you've learned all the ways to minimize your monthly costs and speed your repayment plan, it's time to get serious and start using your own debt planning worksheet, provided at the end of this chapter.

Studiously keeping track of what you pay in principal and interest payments over the course of the year is one surefire way of staying on track with payments. It's also a good deterrent against using more credit. Everyone has to use credit from time to time, but a good rule of thumb is to budget ahead for your needs and not take out loans or use credit for assets that depreciate. Assets or possessions that depreciate, or lose value over time, include clothing, stereos, computers, and even cars. Using credit for assets that have the potential to appreciate or gain value over time, such as home purchases, is acceptable.

In this lesson you learned how to make debt less expensive by finding cheaper credit card rates or consolidating or refinancing your loans and other balances. In the next lesson, you'll learn to calculate how much you should be saving so that you have adequate cash reserves in case of an emergency.

YOUR ANNUAL DEBT PLANNER

	LOANS	CREDIT CARDS
Credit Company Starting Date Total Owed Interest Rate		
Month Amount Paid Interest Late Fee Balance		
Month Amount Paid Interest Late Fee Balance		
Month Amount Paid Interest Late Fee Balance		
Month Amount Paid Interest Late Fee Balance		
Month Amount Paid Interest Late Fee Balance		
Month Amount Paid Interest Late Fee Balance		

	OTHER REVOLVING DEBTS
Credit Company Starting Date Total Owed Interest Rate	
Month Amount Paid Interest Late Fee Balance	
Month Amount Paid Interest Late Fee Balance	
Month Amount Paid Interest Late Fee Balance	
Month Amount Paid Interest Late Fee Balance	
Month Amount Paid Interest Late Fee Balance	
Month Amount Paid Interest Late Fee Balance	

continues

YOUR ANNUAL DEBT PLANNER

	LOANS	CREDIT CARDS
Credit Company Starting Date Total Owed Interest Rate		
Month Amount Paid Interest Late Fee Balance		
Month Amount Paid Interest Late Fee Balance		
Month Amount Paid Interest Late Fee Balance		
Month Amount Paid Interest Late Fee Balance		
Month Amount Paid Interest Late Fee Balance		
Month Amount Paid Interest Late Fee Balance		

OTHER REVOLVING DEBTS

Credit Company
Starting Date
Total Owed
Interest Rate

Month
Amount Paid
Interest
Late Fee
Balance

Month
Amount Paid
Interest
Late Fee
Balance

Month
Amount Paid
Interest
Late Fee
Balance

Month
Amount Paid
Interest
Late Fee
Balance

Month
Amount Paid
Interest
Late Fee
Balance

Month
Amount Paid
Interest
Late Fee
Balance

12

Saving for a Rainy Day

In this lesson you'll learn to calculate how much you should be saving so that you have adequate cash reserves in case of an emergency. You'll also learn about other options you have for financing an emergency shortfall and how to determine the least expensive money available to you.

Protecting Your Future

What would your finances look like if you lost your job tomorrow and couldn't find another one for a month? How about for three months? What would happen if your roof caved in and, even after insurance covered part of the damage, you still owed $2,000? Or worse, what if you were disabled for a year, and couldn't work?

No one likes to think about it, but all of these events are possible. What adds insult to injury during emergencies of this type is that your bills won't stop. You'll still need to buy groceries, pay your rent or mortgage, your car payment, your insurance premiums, and the minimum payments on loans and credit cards. Emergency planning doesn't mean you or even anyone you know will be struck by an emergency next week or even next year. What it means is that you've taken simple steps to ensure that you have a cash cushion in place, come what may. That's why it's called rainy day savings. Hopefully, every day of your future will be sunny. But if it isn't, by putting a simple rainy day savings strategy in place, you'll be prepared.

HOW MUCH DO YOU NEED?

Most money experts agree that keeping a cash reserve of at least three months of expenses is a smart financial planning tool, but you may need more or less depending on your situation. A single person who lives with parents and has few bills does not need as much as the sole breadwinner of a household. The simplest way to determine how much you need is to ask yourself how your bills will get paid if you lose your income. You may need a fatter reserve if your income fluctuates because of your line of work—if you own your own business, depend on sales commissions, or work in a field that is seasonal, such as construction, for example. The same is true if your job stability is uncertain or you're expecting to have to pay for a family member's medical bills or living expenses sometime in the future. You can get by with less of a cash cushion if your household has two incomes or you can easily borrow against assets such as home equity, a retirement plan, or a life insurance policy.

As you figure out how much you would need if an emergency strikes, be realistic about determining which bills could wait and which couldn't. You can always pay the minimum on credit cards, but creditors won't wait very long for mortgage or car payments—usually 60 days or less—before moving to initiate proceedings to foreclose on or repossess what by law is theirs. Do you have enough socked away in a bank account or fairly liquid investment so you can get the cash in a hurry to cover an emergency? Or, can you borrow the money you need in a crunch?

Liquid Investment   A liquid investment or asset is one you can cash out of quickly without paying an early withdrawal penalty. Liquid investments include savings and checking accounts, money market accounts, money market funds, mutual funds, and even stocks and bonds.

If you're fairly typical, accumulating enough cash in rainy day savings to cover three months of expenses should suffice. You can determine your own expenses easily by looking at your monthly budget worksheets and multiplying your overall monthly costs by three. Let's assume your expenses are $1,200 per month and add up to $3,600 for three months. How would you come up with that kind of cash if you were hit with a layoff at work and found yourself suddenly unemployed?

If you have enough savings or have ready access to that kind of cash, congratulate yourself. If, however, you find yourself living paycheck to paycheck, with little left over after your bills are paid and few options for borrowing, don't despair. By evaluating your situation now and determining what your needs might be in an emergency, you can begin to build a cash cushion that will see your through an emergency. But even if you can only tuck away $5 or $10 in savings each payday, start your rainy day savings plan now. If you make savings a regular part of your weekly or monthly activities, you'll be surprised at how quickly your balance will grow. As it does, seek out an account that pays you interest, such as a NOW checking account or money market account, which will help your money grow even faster. If you contribute $40 a month to an account that pays no interest, you'll have $480 at the end of the year. But find an account that pays 5% interest and you'll have $504 after 12 months. The higher the interest rate paid, the more you'll earn.

Although it may not be as alluring as the diamond ring or a cruise around the Greek Isles you're dreaming of, add emergency savings to the list of goals you developed in Lesson 2. With the new entry in your goal worksheet staring you in the face each month, it should serve as a reminder that you need to make disciplined savings part of your financial activities.

Other Means of Emergency Cash

It may be less important to actually save for a rainy day if you have access to other forms of fairly liquid investments or assets. For instance, you can get cash out of money markets, mutual funds, and stocks and bonds, usually within 24 hours, if the need arises. Just be sure to consider all costs.

If your stocks, bonds, mutual funds, or money markets were bought through a broker, you will be charged a commission to sell your investment and, depending on the investment, you may also be charged some sort of exit fee. Some mutual funds, for example, charge investors a redemption fee or a deferred-sales fee (which is charged only in the first five years of an investment) to discourage investors from selling.

Some investments may be harder to sell or, if your emergency occurs at an inopportune time, you may have to sell at a loss. This can be true of mutual funds, stocks, and bonds, whose value fluctuates over time. Other investments such as a bank certificate of deposit may not be a good candidate as potential rainy day savings money because if you cash out before the date the certificate matures, you will be charged an early withdrawal penalty that usually amounts to 5% of your earnings in the course of a year.

Although none of these costs necessarily make your investments a bad source of emergency cash (the commission you pay to sell may be as low as $15), it is important to assess what your actual costs will be before earmarking an asset for rainy day savings.

The good news is, depending on how you invest, you may find you incur no costs to sell investments. For instance, you may be able to sell mutual funds without incurring any kind of sales commission or fee. The same is true of many money market accounts and money market funds, provided you did not buy them through a broker. Some money markets even give you checks you can write, usually for a minimum of $500, which makes accessing your cash that much easier. For more details on sound investing, see Lesson 14.

Just remember, when the emergency is past, start putting the money back into your investments, particularly if they were earmarked for specific goals, such as buying a vacation home or retirement.

Borrowing from Yourself

Borrowing from yourself, either by borrowing from the cash values you've accumulated in an insurance policy, from a retirement plan, or from a home equity line of credit, are also options when an emergency strikes. But again, it is important to weigh the cost of your options and determine whether you can afford to make the additional debt payments you may incur as a result of borrowing.

Life Insurance Loans

Borrowing from a life insurance policy is possible if you've had the policy long enough to accumulate some cash value. But be sure to consider your interest-rate costs. You'll be charged a fixed-rate of about 8% to borrow from a newer policy, with those policies that offer variable rate loans charging slightly more. If you purchased your policy in the mid-1970s or before, you may only be charged between 5% and 6%, which is a bargain compared to the 18% or more you'd pay to take out a cash advance on a credit card. Most policies allow you to borrow up to 95% of the cash values you've accumulated. Check with the insurance company that issued your policy or your insurance agent for specifics.

On the downside of borrowing from a life insurance policy: You'll reduce your policy's death benefit by the amount of the loan.

If possible, consider carefully what slashing your death benefit will mean to members of your household in the event of your demise. Insurance agents routinely tell horror stories about individuals who gutted their insurance policies by taking out huge loans they never repaid, thereby leaving their families with little or nothing when they died. If your family needs the death benefit, find out in writing what it will cost you each month to make the policy whole. Because some insurance companies reduce the interest or dividends they pay on policies with loans, you should also get in writing what impact that will have on your future cash values and the premiums you owe. They may go up as a result of the loan or you may have to pay premiums for a longer period of time than you agreed to when you originally purchased your policy.

RETIREMENT PLAN LOANS

If your employer offers a 401(k) or another type of retirement plan you've contributed to over the years, you may well be able to borrow the tax-deferred investments you've made.

Interest rates for borrowing from your plan generally run in the vicinity of 8% to 10%, but may be higher because employers are only required by the Department of Labor to set a market rate. Repayment of a loan on your retirement plan must be made in full within five years, with the exception of loans made to purchase a home, which can be stretched out 30 years. Federal law limits the size of such loans to 50% of the assets you've accumulated in your plan, because they don't want you to deplete all your retirement savings as a result of borrowing.

In addition to determining whether or not you'll be able to pay back the new loan, there are other long-term costs to consider before borrowing from a retirement plan. While your employer or the administrator of your plan can tell you what interest rate you'll be charged for the borrowing, the true cost for the loan is greater. If you're being charged 7% on the loan, but your money would have earned 12% inside the plan, you're losing out on the additional 5% of interest your money would have been earning. And because, as the old saying goes, it takes money to earn money, by reducing the balance in your retirement plan account, you're actually losing out on the compounding that would have taken place on the amount you borrow.

 Compounding If you invest in an account that pays you interest, compounding is the interest you earn on the interest you've earned.

To minimize this lost earning potential, ask your employer if you can borrow money from the lowest-earning investments in your plan. That way, you'll lose out on the least amount of interest and compounding.

You should also ask whether or not you'll be allowed to contribute to your retirement plan while your loan is outstanding and if the company will continue to make a matching contribution. In some cases, both contributions cease when a loan is taken out. How long will it take you to pay the loan back? If you're in your 40s or older, the interruption in contributions could set your retirement back several years. On the plus side, however, if you can use the contribution you are accustomed to making as your loan payment instead, your monthly budget won't take an additional hit.

You should also be sure you're going to stay with your present employer for the term of repayment. If you leave a company while you still have an outstanding retirement plan loan, you'll have to pay off the loan in full when you quit or the Internal Revenue Service will view the loan as an early withdrawal and you'll be required to pay income taxes and, if you're younger than $59 \frac{1}{2}$ years old, you'll also be charged a 10% penalty on the amount you borrowed.

Borrowing Against Your House

If you own your own home and have built up equity (which means you've either paid off part of your mortgage or the value of your house has increased since you've owned it), you can borrow it either in the form of a loan or a line of credit. If you take out a home loan you'll get a lump sum you can use immediately or deposit in your bank account. A home-equity line of credit is issued in the form of funds you can draw on as you need to, usually by writing checks you're given when you're issued the line of credit. You pay interest on the loan immediately, but will only be charged interest on the line of credit as you use it. If a job layoff or another reason for needing emergency funds is looming, apply for a home-equity loan or line of credit before disaster strikes. Banks will be much less eager to grant you credit if you're unemployed or are already having trouble paying your bills.

You should also keep in mind that the collateral for the loan is your home—you pledge it to the lender as part of the loan deal—and if you miss a payment, the lender can initiate fore-closure proceedings to take possession of it.

Average home equity interest rates range from 8%–10%. Because home-equity loans and lines of credit have become a lucrative business for banks in the past decade, some will waive closing costs and fees and offer you low introductory rates, which can save you hundreds of dollars in fees and inter-est rate charges the first year. For this reason, it's important to shop for a competitive home-equity loan. But be sure to calcu-late what your payments will be once the introductory rate expires—the low rates usually only last three to six months—and make sure you can still afford the monthly payment when it jumps.

Are you planning on selling your home in the near future? An outstanding home-equity loan or line of credit can impact your sale. Say you've managed to accumulate $30,000 in eq-uity in your house and you borrow $20,000. When you sell, you'll have to pay back that $20,000 and if the real estate mar-ket in your area is depressed, you may walk away without any profit or perhaps even be forced take a loss.

The good news is that the interest you pay on up to $100,000 of home-equity debt is tax-deductible when you prepare your income taxes. So if you're in the 28% tax bracket, a 10% home-equity loan translates into a 7.2% rate once you take the income tax deduction. You can usually deduct the interest for state and local tax returns, too.

BORROWING FROM THE BANK

As a last resort, if you run into an emergency and have no place else to turn, you can turn to the bank. Consumer loans, overdraft protection, and credit card advances are three options for cash that may be available to you.

They each have different interest rates and overall costs. For instance, credit card companies routinely tack on a 2% fee when they issue cash advances. So make sure you investigate your options as early as possible when an emergency strikes so you can get the most economical deal. It's also wise to apply for whichever line of credit you opt for as soon as possible, before late payments show up on your credit report and make your chances of getting additional credit slim.

Consumer loan rates run between 13% and 17%, but make sure to check out rates offered by your local credit unions, if you have access to one, because they are routinely 2% to 3% lower than the rates charged by banks. If you have collateral such as real estate, you can opt for a secured loan or line of credit, which also offers cheaper rates.

Credit card cash advances, in addition to the 2% surcharge you'll be charged, have more expensive interest rates of between 16%–21%. The interest-rate charge for overdraft protection, a line of credit that you can attach to your checking account so you can write checks and make withdrawals even when your balance is $0, hovers around 18%. Remember, however, that you must apply for overdraft protection at your bank and the line of credit it extends may only be $500 or $1,000.

OTHER SOLUTIONS

If you run into an emergency, try to be creative before borrowing, especially if there is some chance you may not be able to meet payments on a new loan. If you have assets that are valuable, such as a boat, a second car, or jewelry, consider selling them. A night or weekend job or even a job you procure through a temporary agency if you're unemployed can also go a long way toward making ends meet.

If you have a family member or friend who is willing to make a loan to you, agree to a pay them interest and make sure you can repay the loan in full in a timely fashion. Believe it or not, family and friends are a lot more valuable than money. For that reason, it's a good measure to agree to a repayment plan of a set amount every month and put the deal in writing so there will be no confusion.

Last Resort   Ask a family member or friend for a loan only after you've exhausted all other funding options. Misunderstandings over even small loans can create ill will that lasts years.

Not everyone needs a huge rainy day umbrella, but you should realistically make sure you have enough easily accessible cash to pay your bills if an emergency strikes. Be prepared to fully evaluate the costs of cashing in any investments or taking out a loan against existing assets, or from the bank at less attractive interest rates, to cover expenses.

In this lesson, you determined how much you should be saving as a minimum to be able to cover emergency expenses. You also examined the different options you have for borrowing from yourself or the bank. In the next lesson, you'll learn how to start a reasonable, overall savings plan.

13

START SAVING

In this lesson, you'll learn how to make the act of saving relatively painless and how to get your savings plan underway.

CREATE A SAVINGS PLAN

The whole purpose of budgeting is to give you more money after you pay your bills each month. The next step is to direct that money to savings so you can cover emergencies and achieve goals, whether they include buying a new car, going back to school, or purchasing your dream vacation home.

In Lesson 7, you saw how much you have left over every month, after bills and expenses are deducted from your monthly income. By using a savings worksheet, you'll find it easier to track how much of that cash makes it into savings each month. It's as simple as recording your leftover money, your savings goals, and what you actually save (because the amount differs). The worksheet also gives you a spot to note the reasons for any savings shortfalls you have each month. This will give you a handy reference for readjusting your budget, if you've forgotten or overlooked expenses. It will also serve as a reminder of whether or not you're meeting your savings goals. Here's an example of the Smith family's worksheet.

The Smiths' Savings Goals

Month	Cash After Bills	Savings Goal	Actual Savings	Reason for Shortfall
January	$150	$125	$75	Restaurant meals
Annual Savings Goal			$1,500	
Actual Annual Savings			$_____	

By using the worksheet, the Smiths can see they've gotten their savings plan off to a rocky start. They earmarked $125 for savings, but only managed to tuck away $75. The reason? They spent half of what they were supposed to save at restaurants instead. By recording the reason for the shortfall, they can see that their actions had a direct impact on their savings goals and their overall financial picture. Here's a worksheet you can use to get started on your own savings goals.

Your Savings Worksheet

Month	Cash After Bills	Savings Goal	Actual Savings	Reason for Shortfall
January	_____	_____	_____	_____
February	_____	_____	_____	_____
March	_____	_____	_____	_____
April	_____	_____	_____	_____
May	_____	_____	_____	_____
June	_____	_____	_____	_____
July	_____	_____	_____	_____
August	_____	_____	_____	_____

Month	Cash After Bills	Savings Goal	Actual Savings	Reason for Shortfall
September	_____	_____	_____	_____
October	_____	_____	_____	_____
November	_____	_____	_____	_____
December	_____	_____	_____	_____
Annual Savings Goal			$_____	
Actual Annual Savings			$_____	

Keeping your savings worksheet current is as important as tracking expenses. After all, what you tuck away in savings is your reward for being careful about how you spend your money. Saving is a way of making sure some portion of what you earn hour by hour during the course of your work week goes to you and not just to pay for goods and services.

Your worksheet allows you to see how soundly your household is budgeting and whether or not your reasons for any shortfalls can be attributed to emergencies, overlooked expenses, or just plain overspending. If unforeseen expenses come up month after month, you need to add the items to your monthly budget. If your household is using money on items such as extra games of golf or entertainment, the worksheet will help you pinpoint that and tell you that it's time to apply the spending brakes and inject added discipline into daily spending habits so you can meet your monthly goals in the future.

Setting Your Goal for the Year

The worksheet gives you a long-range view of your savings and how fast they do or do not accumulate, by providing spaces for your annual savings goal and the actual amount you save over the course of the year. In that way, it leaves little room for fudging. You are either on track or you're not and the worksheet tells you that, month by month.

But how much should you save? The question really is, how much *can* you save and how important is it to you? Your decision should be based on three factors: your need for emergency savings, the amount of money it will take to achieve your goals, and how much time you believe is a reasonable period for reaching your goals. You will, of course, want to count any savings you've already accumulated, which will put you that much further ahead of the game.

You learned in Lesson 12 that it is a sound rule of thumb to keep enough savings in reserve to cover at least three months of living expenses, so unless you already have money tucked away, savings you can get at in an emergency should be your number one savings priority. Say that three months of living expenses in your household comes to $3,600 and that the worksheet in Lesson 7 helped you determine that you have $300 left over after all your bills are paid each month. Simple math tells you that it will take you 12 months to save enough to cover three months of living expenses, should an emergency befall you.

But what about your larger goals? How long will it take you to achieve them if you save all of your discretionary income? Maybe you've been dreaming about a two-week trip to Hawaii and you stop by a local travel agent's office and determine it will cost you about $2,400 for airfare, hotel, and food. That's another six months you'll have to save $300 in addition to the year it will take you to accumulate three months of emergency expenses. But if you stay on track, 18 months from now you'll have both an emergency cushion and be packing to take the vacation you've dreamed about.

Eighteen months may seem like a long time, but foregoing emergency savings and putting that dream trip on a credit card would be much more costly.

Your annual savings goal, in this case, should be $3,600, based on the $300 you believe you can tuck away each month. Even if your debt payments and bills allow you to save much less than $300 a month, saving what you can even if it's only $10 or $15 is a great way to get started on a savings plan. The simple truth is, time moves forward whether you save or not. Both budgeting and savings require you to take a long-range view of your finances. It is better to get started on a savings plan of $10 a month today and increase the amount you save as you winnow back your bills than to find yourself without any savings 10 years from now.

Keeping your goals firmly in mind (don't forget to put a picture of your goal on your refrigerator or inside your medicine cabinet as a daily reminder) should persuade you to make up for any monthly shortfall that appears on your savings worksheet. If you run into a shortfall, contribute extra to savings in the months that follow.

TRICKS OF THE TRADE

- *Find the right account.* If you're just getting started saving you may not want to open a separate savings account immediately unless you can find one that won't charge a monthly service fee based on your small balance. That's going to require you to keep your savings in your checking account. To do this successfully, deduct what you're saving from your checking account balance and record it in a separate ledger in the back of your checkbook along with the date of your "deposit" and what your savings balance is. If you're a free-wheeling spender, you must convince yourself that this money is no longer available to you—it's earmarked for your goals. Separating it from your checking account balance should help. Once you safely meet your bank's minimum balance requirement for a free savings account, open one. It will reduce the risk that you'll spend your savings and help you avoid any accounting errors you might make by keeping checking and savings together in one account.

- *Don't leave it to chance.* Unless you're the type of person who will deposit money in a savings account every month come rain, shine, or temptation, make arrangements with your bank to have the money deposited automatically in your savings account. The transaction is called an automatic transfer. By filling out a simple form at your bank, you're telling it to move a set amount of money from your checking account to your savings account on the same day each month. By signing up for your bank's automatic transfer services, you'll ensure that the money makes it into savings and out of temptation in your checking account, whether or not you make it to the bank or the ATM machine to make a deposit. View the transaction as a regular bill—albeit a more pleasant and

productive one than most—and make sure to deduct
the amount from your checking account on the date
you tell the bank to make the transfer. Putting the
deposit on auto-pilot is a surefire way to force yourself
to save. Most banks offer an electronic personal computer banking program and phone banking programs
that allow you to make the transfers yourself for free if
you're disciplined enough.

- *What's your frequency?* If saving on a monthly basis
  doesn't work for you because money sitting in your
  checking account is too much of a temptation, put
  your automatic savings plan on a weekly basis by
  dividing by four the discretionary income you plan
  to save for the month and having your bank transfer
  the money for you each week. If your savings is irregular because of self-employment or another situation, time your savings to take place quarterly. Your
  bank can make the transfers whenever you tell it to
  on the form you fill out. Just make sure to keep track
  of the dates of transfer so you don't forget to record
  the deductions in your checking account.

- *What to do with windfalls.* If you get a bonus at work
  or an income tax refund that's not specifically earmarked for an emergency such as a car repair or
  doctor's bill, put the money directly into savings.
  The same rule applies to any raises you get at work or
  any extra income you earn doing side jobs or free-
  lance work. By making it a practice to put "found"
  money directly into your savings account, you'll
  reach your goals that much quicker.

- Find the best interest rate. Once your savings account starts to grow, try to find a checking account
  that pays interest. Most banks offer an interest-
  bearing NOW account, but be certain you meet their
  minimum balance requirement or any interest you
  earn will be drained away in monthly fees. Or consider moving your emergency fund it into the
  highest-yielding short-term money market account
  offered by a bank in your area. You'll earn interest
  and the money is federally insured against the type
  of losses you might experience if you put the money
  into a stock or bond mutual fund. At the same time,
  unlike a certificate of deposit (CD), which requires
  you to pay an early withdrawal penalty unless you
  leave your money on deposit for a set period of time
  (depending on the CD you choose, usually between
  30 days and five years), you'll be able to make deposits and withdraw your money from most bank
  money market accounts without penalty. Many even
  offer check-writing privileges, but if you're the type
  who may be tempted to write checks for whimsical
  purchases, refuse the check option. You make withdrawals when you need to by visiting a branch anyway.

In this lesson you learned how to start a fee-free, regular savings plan, put it on auto-pilot, and minimize the temptation
to raid what you accumulate. In the next lesson, you'll learn to
determine how much money you will need to live comfortably
in retirement and take advantage of retirement plans and individual retirement accounts.

Understanding the Retirement Puzzle

In this lesson you'll learn to determine how much money you will need to live comfortably in retirement and how much you can expect from Social Security. You'll also learn how to take full advantage of retirement plans and individual retirement accounts and adopt a plan to close any savings gap.

How Much Will You Need to Retire?

That question depends on what lifestyle you're shooting for. If you want to live comfortably in retirement you will need between 50% and 70% of your pre-retirement income every year you plan to spend retired. If, on the other hand, you're planning lavish expenses like buying a second home (without selling the first one) and extensive and frequent exotic travel, you'll need 80% or more of your present income every year you're retired. As life expectancies increase, you may find yourself spending 20 or more years in retirement.

Say you expect to pay off your home mortgage—a major expense now—by the time you're 60 and work until you're 65 and believe you'll need 60% of your current earnings every year you're retired after that. Simply multiply your current income—say it's $35,000—by 60%. This reveals you will need $21,000 a year to live comfortably in retirement.

Don't Forget Taxes

Now multiply that amount by 25% to take taxes into consideration (if you know your tax rate will be higher, use a higher number). The result, using these numbers, is that you will need $5,250 more than $21,000 to ensure you can afford state and federal income taxes. Under this given scenario, your tab to maintain your lifestyle in retirement will be $26,250 a year.

What About Inflation?

Most financial planners and money experts predict that inflation will increase about 3% a year. So how will that increase the $26,250 you'll need every year to support your retirement? Put another way, what do you need in this year's dollars by the time you're 65? To find that, you'll need to calculate your monthly income. If you divide $26,250 by 12, to determine what your monthly income will need to be, you arrive at $2,187.50. Then decide how many years you have until retirement. After that, you select the corresponding inflation factor from the following table. That number will tell you what you'll actually need each month when you retire.

Inflation Inflation is the rate at which prices on goods and services will increase each year, thereby eroding the purchasing power of today's dollar.

Say you have 15 years until retirement. Multiply your projected monthly retirement income of $2,187.50 by the inflation factor that corresponds to the number of years you have until retirement. For 15 years the inflation factor is 1.81%. The calculation reveals you will need $3,412.50 in monthly income 15 years from now to buy what $2,187.50 can purchase today. Here's the math:

TABLE 14.1 FIGURING HOW INFLATION WILL AFFECT YOUR RETIREMENT SAVINGS

Projected monthly retirement income needed	$2,187.50
Inflation factor for 15 years until retirement	× 1.56
Inflation-adjusted monthly retirement income:	$3,412.50

Choose your own inflation factor from the following table to determine how much you will need to live comfortably each month.

TABLE 14.2 INFLATION FACTORS

NUMBER OF YEARS UNTIL RETIREMENT	INFLATION FACTOR
5	1.16%
10	1.34%
15	1.56%
20	1.81%
25	2.09%
30	2.43%
35	2.81%
40	3.26%

WHERE WILL YOUR MONEY COME FROM?

Before you panic at the inflation-adjusted monthly income you'll need in retirement, realize that if you work now you will have at least one source of retirement income. Despite dire predictions, you will receive Social Security benefits. You may also have a pension or retirement plan at work or maybe you've started an individual retirement account (IRA)—all three of which let you invest money tax-free until you start drawing on your funds in retirement. You may also have a spouse's pension or retirement plan to take into consideration (and their Social Security). Or maybe you're planning to start an IRA or begin contributing to a retirement plan at work.

You should also ask yourself if you can expect to inherit property, cash, investments, or all three. Last, but certainly not least, you actually might want to work at least part-time in retirement, which will also add to your monthly income.

To fully explore your options and see how much, if any, you can expect to get from each of the above sources of retirement income, let's look at them separately so you can calculate what you count toward monthly retirement income and what you will need to supplement through savings and investments.

WHAT WILL YOU GET FROM SOCIAL SECURITY?

No one can tell you that, except the Social Security Administration, since the agency is supposed to keep track of every dollar you and your employer are taxed (you and an employer each pay half of the 12.4% tax on what you earn each year) to fund your Social Security benefit. If you're self-employed, you pay the entire tab yourself.

The agency calculates benefits based on your highest 35 years' earnings. You can obtain an estimate of your benefits by calling the Social Security Administration at 800-772-1213. If you earned between $35,000 and $50,000, or expect to, for 35 years, you can count on benefits of between $800 and $1,100 a month if you retire between age 65 and 67, but call the agency to be sure. If you retire early, at age 62, your benefits will be reduced.

FREE MONEY FROM YOUR EMPLOYER

If your employer offers a pension plan, you're probably automatically enrolled. That means they put money in an investment account for you. The amount they contribute is based on a percentage of your salary. You may not receive full funding from your employer until you have worked for your company from between four to seven years (called the vesting period). Your employee benefits or human resources department can tell you what you can expect to get in a monthly pension benefit. Pension plans are managed by money managers who decide how to invest the funds and you will not be given an opportunity to make investment choices.

Your job may also, or alternatively, offer a defined contribution plan (called a 401(k) plan in the private sector and a 403(b) plan if you work for the local, state, or federal government). This type of plan allows you to determine what percentage of your salary (up to a maximum of 15%) you want to contribute every year. Often, such plans include an employer-match, which means if you contribute a certain amount your company will match some portion of that. Their match, however, will not become fully available to you when you retire unless you're employed by the company a certain number of years (usually between five and seven years). That's free money from your company and you should take advantage of it by investing at least as much as you need to get the maximum contribution from your company.

Defined contribution plans also give you the opportunity to invest your funds in a choice of investments your company selected for the plan. Such investment options usually include several stock mutual funds, one or two bond mutual funds, a money market fund, and an international fund (for tips on choosing investments, turn to Lesson 15).

We'll soon look at the advantages of investing money in a tax-deferred account such as a defined contribution plan, but there is another chief tax advantage to 401(k) or 403(b) investing you should consider. Every dollar you invest, up to 15%, is money that is deducted from your gross income for purposes of determining how much state and federal income tax you owe. Investing even 5% or 6% in a defined contribution plan shaves that much off how much income the IRS can look at when taxing you. On top of being a great way to provide for retirement income—plans will automatically make the deduction for you—this is a no-brainer way to reduce your income taxes.

Your company, or the investment company your employer works with, can you give you an estimate on what your monthly income from such a plan will be based on your contribution, any employer match, and whether or not you are likely to be fully vested.

INDIVIDUAL RETIREMENT ACCOUNTS

Even if your company doesn't offer a retirement plan, or you're self-employed, you can still do your own retirement investing through an IRA. As in a retirement plan at work, earnings accumulate in an IRA tax-deferred account, which means you won't pay taxes until you make withdrawals after age 59 1/2, the earliest age you can start making withdrawals without pen-alty. If you take your money out earlier, you'll pay full income taxes on your earnings and a 10% penalty, so make sure the money you put in an IRA is clearly earmarked for retirement.

If you're single and make less than $35,000 and don't contrib-ute to a plan at work, you're entitled to invest up to $2,000 a year in an IRA and deduct that amount from your gross earn-ings when you file your income tax return. If you're married, file jointly, and earn less than $50,000 as a couple, you can con-tribute up to $4,000 to your IRA and shave the contribution off your gross income for tax purposes. That means you'll pay less income tax or, if you're entitled to money back, your refund will be larger.

So what do you put in an IRA and where do you get one? Think of an IRA as the wrapper, almost like an eggroll wrapper, that lets the IRS know this is money you're investing for retirement. You can put any investment inside an IRA that you like, includ-ing stock mutual funds and bond mutual funds.

If you're just getting started, steer clear of IRAs that require sub-stantial minimum investments or charge high fees or sales com-missions. Instead, work with a reputable no-load (this means no-fee) mutual fund company that allows you pick from the entire menu of their investment offerings. Even if you select only one stock fund or a more conservative money market ac-count (for details on risks and rewards, see Lesson 15) that has performed well for the past 10 years, there are fund companies that allow you to set up an IRA if you sign up to have as little as $50 or $100 a month transferred directly from your checking account. They'll also send you monthly performance state-ments, so you can watch your earnings grow over time. Three reputable companies offering IRAs include T. Rowe Price (800-638-5660), Berger Associates (800-333-1001), and Strong Capital Management (800-368-3863).

These or any company you work with should be able to tell
you what you'll accumulate in your IRA based on your contributions and an estimate that you'll earn between 8% and 10%
on your money each year.

THE BEAUTY OF TAX-DEFERRED INVESTING

Besides being able to deduct what you contribute to an IRA or
a work retirement plan from your gross income for tax purposes every year, the other chief tax benefit of investing this
way is that your earnings will grow tax-free until you start
making withdrawals when you retire. Simply put, your money
grows faster when it is not taxed.

The following table shows how beneficial tax-deferred savings
can be. It assumes you contribute $2,000 a year and your in-
vestments earn an 8% average annual rate of return and shows
the difference in how your money will grow in a tax-deferred
investment and a taxable investment.

TABLE 14.3   HOW TAX-DEFERRED INVESTING WORKS

YEARS	5	10	15	20	25	30
Tax-deferred	$12,672	$31,291	$58,649	$98,846	$157,909	$244,692
Taxable	$11,846	$27,475	$48,096	$75,303	$111,200	$158,562

When you look at the table you can see that the benefits of
investing inside a retirement plan or an IRA you start yourself
are clear, especially over the long-term. Your money grows
faster, especially over the long-term, when it is shielded from
the taxes you would otherwise pay on returns.

WHAT WILL YOU INHERIT?

If you have no family or close friends who are likely to leave you anything, read no further. But if your parents or grandparents have given you a copy of their will and have named you a beneficiary of an insurance policy or plan to leave you, and maybe your siblings, other investments or even a house, you can count these assets toward income you can expect to have in retirement. Of course, that means you can't spend whatever windfall you receive now. You have to save or invest it for retirement.

FINDING MONEY IN A TIGHT BUDGET

Retirement can seem like a long way off, especially if it really is a decade or more away, but Table 14.2 demonstrates that your money needs to grow. Start small if you have to, but start saving for retirement as soon as possible if you haven't already done so.

If you're on a tight budget today, but can foresee having some extra cash as you pay off bills in the near future, write a date on your calendar as a deadline for getting started and stick to it. If you get a raise at work or come into money as a result of a tax return or some other source, use it to invest for retirement.

If you don't foresee having any available cash in the short-term, it may be time to do away with some item in your weekly or monthly expenses that is dispensable, even it means taking a one-week vacation instead of a two-week vacation this year.

In this lesson you learned how to calculate what you will need to save to live comfortably in retirement, taking into consideration what you can expect from Social Security benefits, your retirement savings, and any inheritance you may have coming. In the next lesson, you'll learn how to make investing an easy and fairly painless process.

15

SOUND RULES FOR EASY INVESTING

In this lesson you'll learn simple rules for developing an effective, long-term investment plan and choosing sound investments. You'll also learn about risks and rewards.

INVESTING MADE EASY

If you're new to the world of investing, the overload of confusing information regarding what you should and should not do with your money can be enough to make you stick your hard-earned cash under your mattress and forget about it. But investing, even if you have hundreds of thousands of dollars sitting under that mattress, doesn't need to be brain surgery. There are some simple facts you need to consider before you get started and some misconceptions and pitfalls to avoid. But beyond that, investing can be an easy process.

Investing starts with a simple first step you've learned all about in this book: finding money you can dedicate to investment each month. If you're not putting anything aside for retirement yet, by all means start your investment plan first by putting money in a retirement plan offered at your place of work or by starting an IRA (for details, see Lesson 14). But if you already have your retirement bases pretty well covered, it's time to start building a simple investment portfolio you can use to finance a dream or two before you retire.

 Portfolio A portfolio is simply the imaginary line you draw around all of your investments and savings, including retirement investments, so that you look at your investments in terms of performance, risk, the areas of the market you're investing in, and what you're worth overall.

Saving in a bank savings account is fine, especially if it's emergency savings or money you want to use this year or in the next five years. But as you find more money you'd like to put to work for you and can keep it tucked away for five years or more, it's important to maximize your earning potential through investing.

Over the past 20 years, the stock market has given investors historical annual average returns of 10%. That's a good deal more than you can earn under your mattress or in a bank account. The following table illustrates what $1,000 a year will earn under different interest rate scenarios.

TABLE 15.1 HOW YOUR MONEY GROWS

YEARS INVESTED	TOTAL INVESTED	5%	10%	15%
5	$5,000	$5,802	$6,716	$7,754
10	$10,000	$13,207	$17,531	$ 23,349
15	$15,000	$22,657	$34,950	$ 54,717
20	$20,000	$34,719	$63,002	$117,810

START WITH A MUTUAL FUND

If you're an investment pro, you may know how to evaluate whether an individual company's stock is a good or bad deal, or whether a bond is a good fit for your portfolio. But when you're just getting started you want to diversify and minimize your risk, and a mutual fund does that by investing in a number of company stocks or government bonds or both. You're not depending on one company's success or one government's money management prowess when you invest in a mutual fund. The risk, that the underlying companies or entities will perform well or poorly is spread out among a number of stocks or bonds. So in that sense, even when you invest in only one mutual fund, you get an entire portfolio of stocks or bonds. This allows you to hedge your bet.

On top of that, you get professional money management. The money manager or team of managers that manages the mutual fund you invest in evaluates the performance of each of their investments daily to make sure they are on target. Unless you feel capable of doing this with a host of different individual stocks and bonds, and you have the time, it's best to leave this kind of management to the professionals who are trained and paid to do it. But before you get started, consider the basic principles of investing so you can decide what mutual fund best suits your goals.

THE RULES OF THE ROAD

- *What's your time frame?* Decide how long you plan to invest and for what purpose. There is risk attached to putting your money in mutual funds that can be smoothed out if you leave your money in a mutual fund over time. But if you need the money within the next five years, stick to a money market account or money market mutual fund where you can earn slightly higher than what you'll get from a bank account or certificate of deposit without incurring significant risk that you'll lose the principal amount you're investing.

- *Look at historical performance.* There are a number of different mutual funds available to you and some have spectacular performances in the course of a year, earning investors 30% or more. But you're not investing for one year. Find a fund that has performed well over the course of at least five years (preferably 10 years). Mutual funds, by law, are required to send you performance data and a prospectus that explains the purpose of the fund and its money managers' philosophy. With a long track record, you can see how a fund performed during the volatile market periods, the most recent being 1987 and 1991. If the materials a fund company sends you don't show you how well the fund fared compared to other funds that share its investment goals, go to the library and ask for copies of *MorningStar* and *Valueline.* Both companies publish reports that track the performance of each universe of mutual funds and analyze individual funds' performance within their universe.

- *Evaluate risk and reward.* The rule of thumb for evaluating risk is: The higher reward, the greater the risk you incur that you'll lose your money. Once you wander outside the confines of your bank's savings products, there are no guarantees you'll earn money and none you won't lose money. If you invest in the stock or bond market, even through mutual funds, you can lose money. That's why you need a longer-term investing time horizon. Both *MorningStar* and *Valueline* rate each mutual fund based on how risky a fund is compared to the other funds in its category. Find a fund with average risk.

- *Stock or bond fund?* Stocks and bonds generally have an inverse relationship to interest rates. As interest rates rise, bonds usually decrease in value as stocks increase. That's why both stock and bond mutual funds will eventually play a role in your portfolio. Historically, however, large-company stock funds have earned investors about 12% average annual returns compared to long-term bond funds' 6% average annual returns. The rule of thumb for deciding how much of your overall investment money to put in a stock or bond fund is: Subtract your age from 100 and invest the sum in stock funds. If you're 40, 60% of your investment funds should go in stock mutual funds and 40% in bond funds. Bond funds can act as a hedge against losses if stock mutual funds start to decline.

- *Which type of fund first?* Start with a large company stock fund and build from there. While this type of fund's performance has been slightly lower than small company stock funds over the years, you'll be able to find a large company stock fund with lower risk than those offered in the small-company arena. You can find the universe of large-company stock mutual funds listed, along with their historical performance, in both *MorningStar* and *Valueline* reports. A large-company mutual fund that has returned 13% to 14% over the years is a fine bet. Look at five- and 10-year performance, but also look year-by-year. You might see a relatively large decline in the fund's performance, especially during 1987 or 1991, when the stock market dipped. Was the fund's loss larger, smaller, or about average when compared to other funds in its category? If you have questions about performance, call the fund company and ask.

- *Diversify as you go.* Different sectors of the market, such as large-company stock mutual funds and small-company stock funds, can react differently in different kinds of markets. The same is true for international funds and bond funds. That's why you want to diversify. The hope is that if one sector of the market is down, other sectors you invest in through your mutual funds will not be.

So even if you take a loss in one fund for a year, you may have gains in your other funds if you diversify. As you gain investment momentum and a comfort level, you will want at least four types of mutual funds in your portfolio: a large-company stock fund, a small-company stock fund, an international fund, and a bond fund.

- *Choose a no-load mutual fund.* It's especially true when you're just getting started. You don't want large sums of your hard-earned investment money going to sales commissions. With a minimum of homework on your part you can find a mutual fund that has performed well over the past decade and charges you a minimum of fees. Also opt for an open-end mutual fund, which allows you to buy and sell shares when you want to, usually within 24 hours of notifying the fund company by phone. A closed-end mutual fund issues a predetermined number of shares that trade, as many stocks do, on the New York Stock Exchange, so you will need to engage a broker and pay a sales commission to buy and sell a closed-end fund.

- *Auto-pilot investing.* Numerous no-load mutual funds let you invest as little as $50 or $100 a month if you put your account with them on auto-pilot and set up an automatic transfer from your checking account each month. This is called the dollar-cost averaging method of investing. By investing monthly you buy when the price of mutual fund shares is high and low over a period of time, so this purchase method evens out fluctuations in price. You avoid the risk of investing a large sum just before there is a major drop in price.

YOUR FIRST STEP

As you search for a sound large-company stock mutual fund to invest in, by all means visit the library so you have access to *MorningStar* and *Valueline* reports, both of which do quarterly studies of the top-performing large-company mutual funds. But remember, you're not looking for the "hottest" new fund because it is basically untested. You're looking for a mutual fund that has long-term, consistent performance and has weathered adverse market conditions over the years.

As you narrow your list, ask friends and neighbors where they're investing. Don't let them convince you to invest in a speculative fund with no track record, but at the same time, if your own research bears out their findings, sharing information this way can help you find sound investments.

In this lesson you learned how to evaluate investments and get started on a sound, diversified investment program using mutual funds. In the next lesson, you'll learn how to evaluate your spending and lifestyle choices as budgeting becomes a way of life.

16

CREATIVE LIFESTYLES AND MONEY CHOICES

In this lesson, you'll learn how to avoid money stress by thinking about the options budgeting gives you. You'll also learn to evaluate your spending and lifestyle choices in light of your goals and dreams.

GET YOUR THINKING RIGHT

Sound budgeting means living beneath, not beyond, your means for a lifetime. It doesn't mean earning more money, it means finding more money to use for your dreams. That may call for some creative thinking and choices. You've probably already learned that spending at whim, whenever the mood strikes, only guarantees debt. It doesn't ensure satisfaction or budgeting success.

But if giving up excess spending can be viewed like any habit, for instance eating too many sweets, it's easy to see that you will need to find healthy substitutes for any bad habits you or members of your household are trying to rid themselves of. View these substitutes as a means to a richer life. After all, by creating and sticking to a serious budget that has your goals and dreams as its underpinning, you're making choices and changes that will enhance the rest of your life and put you in control of your financial destiny.

Substituting healthy money habits for poor ones can take many forms. Maybe staying out of restaurants or declaring a moratorium on watching videos at home will give you time to pursue a long-dormant hobby or become an expert in an area that always interested you, such as painting or gardening.

As you pare back overspending, it's time to realize that you don't need to see two $7 movies, go to a basketball game, and eat three meals out (or more) in the course of one weekend to have a good time. There are probably many weekends during which you've crammed in every activity only to discover by Sunday night you're more tired and stressed than you were when you left work Friday afternoon. Good budgeting is about quality, not quantity, and finding affordable ways for you and your household to spend its time can become an enjoyable hobby in itself.

If It's Worth Having, It's Worth Planning For

If you're like many people, your free time has become a finite resource into which you try to fit every type of enjoyment. But planning for that enjoyment often takes a back seat to the actual daily necessities of living and working. Lack of planning can mean a more expensive lifestyle in many ways. Here are some examples of how:

- You know for months that you want to travel on Memorial Day but wait until Monday of that week to buy airfare to the beach.

  Cost: $500 (instead of $189 if you booked 30 days in advance or $269 if you booked 14 days in advance).

- You invite friends over for a Sunday cookout, but wait until an hour before they show up to shop for groceries.

  Cost: $80 (for hot dogs, burgers and chips, because you don't have time to go across town and buy the spareribs that are on sale and marinate them before guests arrive).

- You've been planning for months to start bringing your lunch to work, but instead end up eating in the local deli near your office.

  Cost: $7 a day, $35 a week, $1,820 a year (all because you can't spare five minutes a day to pack a sandwich, fruit, and drink).

Habits have a way of creeping up on all of us. Now is the time to put the brakes on them and take a deep breath. Sometimes as little as 10 or 20 minutes dedicated to planning each week will help you make the most of your free time in a way that might net you both a saner existence and the savings you've been looking for to start an investment plan.

OPEN YOUR HORIZONS

There are more sources for fun and relaxation right around the corner than think. Make it a priority to find freebies that interest you. And if you're struggling to find more money in your budget each month, or just want a saner plan for weekends, start planning your recreation and enjoyment time in the calendar so you don't forget about events in the weeks or months ahead. In the meantime, consider some of the free events that take place, or can take place if you make the plans, everywhere in the country:

- *Picnics*. Make sandwiches and bring a decent bottle of wine or cider and a friend. Find a particularly breathtaking vista near your home and relax. Bring a book or the newspaper, if you never get to read, and just be lazy. Or if you prefer more activity, tell 10 or 20 friends to bring their lunch or dinner and meet in the park for a fast-paced game of volleyball or basketball next weekend. A good turnout might mean your picnic idea becomes a regular event.

- *Free concerts*. If you live in a city, check out the arts and entertainment or weekend section of your newspaper to see if any of the high schools, colleges, or universities in your area plan to play for free any time soon.

- *Museums*. The same section of the newspaper will tell you about new exhibits or gallery openings that may interest you, whether your passion is textiles, photography, the old masters, or sports memorabilia. Some museums charge an entrance fee, but many are free, or at least offer free entrance on occasion. If you find a particular museum that fascinates you, volunteer. You might end up with a second job you like better than your first one.

- *Libraries*. Libraries? You'd be amazed at the offerings some libraries stock—from audio tapes of bestsellers to how-to and travel videos that can make planning a home repair or trip easier. They can be great places, too, for kids to spend a rainy Saturday afternoon. Many libraries also offer meet-the-author nights and have details about book clubs and writer's chat sessions. And it sure beats shelling out $18 or more for new books you can't wait to read. If you're a budding writer or love science fiction so much you just have to find someone else to chat with, bookstores can be a great source of information, too.

- *Festivals.* Festivals catering to the whims of specialized groups ranging from Civil War history buffs to China doll lovers abound and may be free or charge just a few dollars to let you wander among the sights and sounds you love. Hobbies, crafts, and antiques are mainstays of the show and festival circuit. But don't forget food and wine festivals. Sometimes free samples are thrown in for good measure, so watch your newspaper's listings.

- *Historical tours.* Each area of the country has its own history, and historical societies are great places to find out what peculiar or spectacular events took place in or around your neighborhood. They're all great sources of historical tours, which can include home tours, cemetery tours or tours, of surrounding historical sites.

- *Group sports.* There may be competitive or laid-back games of tennis, volleyball, basketball, or softball going on every weekend. And the teams may be looking for new members. It can be fun to watch and even more fun to play. If your local newspaper doesn't list the sports clubs in your area, try the local high school, where some of the teams may meet each week.

- *Seasonal offerings.* Don't forget to take advantage of the seasons in your state, whether that means walking through the forest as autumn burnishes the leaves or swimming in the lake, ocean, or your neighborhood pool during the dog days of summer.

- *Holiday freebies.* During the Christmas season, cities and towns offer free concerts and plays. Halloween usually means a haunted house tour. And don't forget parades and pageants, especially if you have kids to occupy or entertain.

What particular sights does your neck of the woods have to offer? Cities, suburbs, and rural areas each have unique offerings that those of us who live there often overlook. Make it your business to find out what your neighborhood, city, and surrounding areas have in the way of history, art, entertainment, sports events, flea markets, and festivals, and you'll be able to plan your weekends around low- or no-cost events weeks and even months in advance.

FIND GOOD SOURCES

The local newspaper, in the back of a particular section each week, might list every gardening event or horse show within a 200-mile radius. Maybe that's something you've managed to overlook for years. The magazine that caters to your state or city might print every possible singles event or volleyball game going on during each month. Don't ignore the "alternative" newspapers and smaller weeklies that pop up in coffee shops or near the grocery store or bus stop. They might contain news about clubs that are flourishing right under your nose. Who better to ask about activities, places, and events you're interested in than people who make it their hobby to know about these things?

As you clue into the best sources of information for events and news about your interests, don't hesitate to pick up the phone and call the president of a club or an expert whose name you see mentioned in the news or that you've run across in your reading. They, too, could become excellent sources and could turn you on to worlds of information and social interaction that you didn't know existed in your area of interest.

If you're drawing a blank or are determined to find out more about what your area has to offer, try your local library and the libraries at any of colleges or universities near you. Librarians are usually keyed in to a vast array of information the rest of us don't know exists. They might point you to a resource that could change the shape of your weekends (and maybe even weeknights, too) for weeks or even months to come.

MORE SERIOUS MEANS OF COST-CUTTING

Planning your resources, both time and money, doesn't need to be a painful experience. Sometimes it just takes some getting used to and if you keep your goals in mind, your healthy choices should become second nature. The budget success you're sure to encounter if you keep your eye on your expenses and cut back on unnecessary items will be icing on the cake.

Up until now in this lesson, we've talked about the lighter side of cost-cutting. But it may help you to consider areas in your life that are still plaguing your budget. Maybe it's your housing expense or the two or three cars your family has to maintain and pay auto insurance premiums for. Or maybe it's the adult son or daughter who has returned home and isn't quite pulling their weight financially. If some expense is still sapping an inordinate amount of your monthly income, remember that a little creativity and flexibility can go a long way toward shaving unwanted costs from your monthly expenses. Here are some of the most likely candidates for the more serious cost-cutting you may be seeking, along with ways to find additional cash each month:

- *Slash transportation costs.* Use one car instead of two, or if you live in a city, consider using public transportation more often. Sometimes renting a car for a

monthly outing can be much less expensive than car
and insurance payments and maintenance costs.

- *Buy a used car.* If your current car is an old stinker
  that breaks down more than it runs, but you need a
  car for work and errands, consider buying a used
  vehicle. You can buy cheaper from individuals, but if
  you buy from a car dealership, make sure to get a
  decent one- or two-year warranty, so you'll have
  recourse if something breaks. Buying a decent used
  car can be a good stop-gap measure if you're saving
  for a new car, or it can be a pragmatic alternative to
  the cost of high car payments if you haven't budgeted ahead to make a car purchase.

- *Sell your house.* Maybe a divorce settlement or the
  death of a family member has left you with a mortgage payment that practically breaks your budget
  each month. Or maybe you bought your home before you realistically assessed your goals and what
  you could afford to spend. In either event, if you can
  find a place to rent that saves you a significant sum
  each month, consider renting.

- *Take in a boarder.* If you have the space and need the
  extra cash, consider renting an extra room in your
  home to a boarder. To protect yourself, get references
  from any likely candidate and check them out. Make
  sure to have them sign a rental agreement. Most sta-
  tionery stores offer legal rental agreements or you
  can get one from a local real estate agent or landlord.
  They might also have ideas about what you can rea-
  sonably charge and what extra costs you might
  factor in, such as utilities, when determining what a
  fair rent is. Before you put an ad in a newspaper,
  consider asking friends, family members, and
  co-workers if they know anyone who might be

interested in renting your space. It's better to rent to someone you know, even if it's only through acquaintances, and it will save you advertising costs.

- *Charge your child.* If an adult child lives with you or moved back home after time away, it may be time to start charging him or her rent. You can negotiate a fair rent and may want to tack on an extra charge for groceries and phone bills, or tabulate and charge for these amenities separately. It will help teach a young adult the value of a dollar and free up your own budget so you'll have more money to put toward your goals.

- *Get a second job.* In an ideal world, you will devote every penny you earn from a second job to retirement and personal investment. In the real world, you may need the income to pay monthly bills or pare down debt. Whatever you choose to do, try to maximize your earning ability by utilizing your talents. You may earn more preparing one résumé for a neighborhood college graduate in a week than you would stocking shelves at the grocery store in a weekend. Think about what you can do to capitalize on your earning potential. You should also minimize costs. If you'll need to pay a baby-sitter to mind your kids if you go to work, establish a Saturday baby-sitting service so other time-pressed families can pay you for your services. Above all else, make sure the extra income is used for its designated purpose, whether it's paying bills or going into savings, so you don't find yourself every bit as financially strapped months from now.

In this lesson you learned how to use both your time and money in a more meaningful way and how to make lifestyle choices that advance your budgeting goals.

INDEX